STEPHEN RECKER'S

VIRTUAL ★★★ *Gettysburg*™

TEXT BY GARY KROSS

TRANSCRIBED FROM TOURS RECORDED LIVE ON THE GETTYSBURG BATTLE-FIELD

EDITED FOR PRINT BY
ANTIGONI LADD AND STEPHEN RECKER

PUBLISHED BY
ANOTHER SOFTWARE MIRACLE

ISBN 0-9715486-1-7

BATTLE-FIELD OF GETTYSBURG

BATTLE OF GETTYSBURG

VIRTUAL ★★★ *Gettysburg*
STEPHEN RECKER'S

CONTENTS

Audio 1 Tour

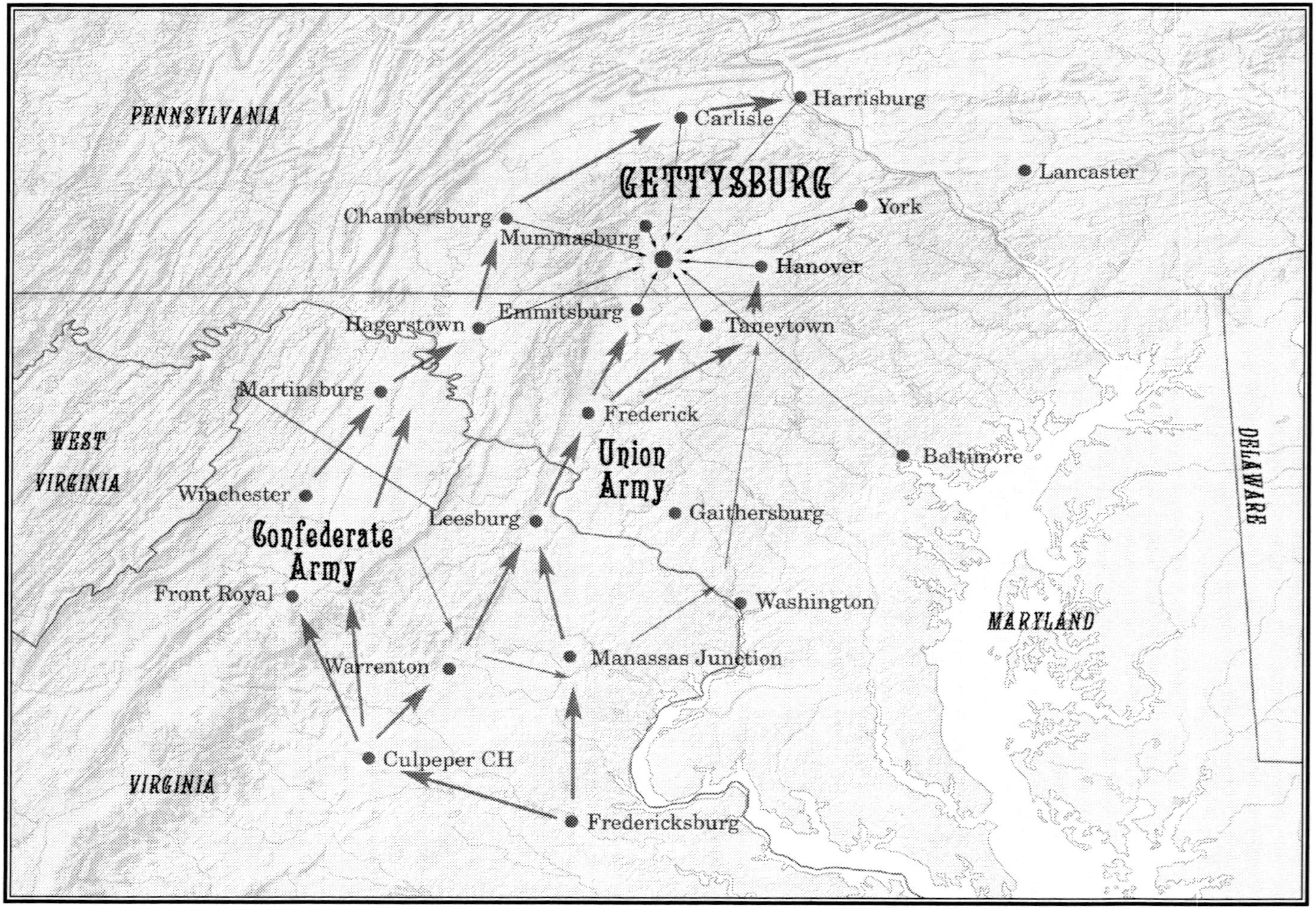

PENNSYLVANIA

Harrisburg

Carlisle

Lancaster

GETTYSBURG

Chambersburg

York

Mummasburg

Hanover

Emmitsburg

Hagerstown

Taneytown

Martinsburg

Frederick

WEST
VIRGINIA

Union
Army

Winchester

Baltimore

Leesburg

DELAWARE

Confederate
Army

Gaithersburg

Front Royal

MARYLAND

Washington

Warrenton

Manassas Junction

Culpeper CH

VIRGINIA

Fredericksburg

~ Prelude to the Battle ~
THE GETTYSBURG CAMPAIGN • JUNE 1863

The Battle of Gettysburg was a three-day battle—July 1st, 2nd, and 3rd, 1863. It was not the *first* battle of the American Civil War; it was certainly not the *last* battle of the American Civil War, but it was the turning point. Both sides knew it would be. That's why the fighting was so vicious.

In three days you would have almost 51,000 American casualties—23,000 Union, 28,000 Confederate. That's 11,000 dead men, 26,000 wounded men that did recover, and 14,000 men captured or listed as missing in action.

The population of the town of Gettysburg was only about 2,400 people at the time of the battle. Why then, was the greatest battle ever fought on the North American continent fought in this little town with a population of 2,400, mostly German immigrants?

The reason is—because of Gettysburg's road system. There are ten main roads that come into Gettysburg from all different directions, like the hub of a wheel. Road systems are incredibly important to Civil War armies. They march from one place to another by road, and there are just so many men you can place on each road. For instance, for every 10,000 men that march down a road—four abreast with all their artillery, their support and their cattle trains—you need anywhere from 14 to 30 miles of road to accommodate that body of men. Contrary to what most people believe about this Civil War site—or any other Civil War site in this country—armies generally do not come up to these battlefields in huge masses. You can't find that many parallel roads leading anywhere in 1863—you still can't, not around here.

ROBERT E. LEE, CSA

The last week of June 1863 finds the Confederate Army—the Army of Northern Virginia—under the command of General Robert E. Lee. This is one of 22 Confederate armies operating in the American Civil War. Lee finds his Confederate army spread over a 55-mile area of south central Pennsylvania. The Union Army, under the command of Major General George Gordon Meade, is the Army of the Potomac, one of 16 Union armies operating in the American Civil War. Meade's army is spread over an area of almost 42 miles in northern Maryland, from flank to flank.

GEORGE G. MEADE, USA

Now both of these armies are looking for a place to concentrate, to come together. On the 28th of June, Robert E. Lee is informed by a Confederate spy—Henry Harrison—that the Union army is coming out of Virginia after him. The Union forces have crossed the Potomac River and are now in northern Maryland, orchestrating to do battle against Lee. Meanwhile Lee finds his army greatly scattered over this 55-mile area of south central Pennsylvania. He needs a place to bring his army together, to concentrate his forces. On the afternoon of the 28th of June, he opens his campaign map, sees a small dot on the map—Gettysburg, with these ten roads leading into it from all different directions—and calls for a general concentration, or a coming together of his Confederate forces. Two-and-a-half days before the Battle of Gettysburg, you have Confederates with marching orders to the Gettysburg area.

The very next day, on the morning of the 29th of June, George Gordon Meade, the Union commander, sees his army spread over a 42-mile area of northern Maryland. He realizes that Lee is up ahead somewhere. He needs a place to draw his army together, and quite by happenstance—again because of the road system of Gettysburg—he chooses Gettysburg as a point of Union concentration.

Neither general knows what the other general is doing, and quite by happenstance they pick the same place to concentrate their forces. In fact, this is the only battle ever fought

HENRY HARRISON, SPY

in the American Civil War where both armies met on the march. They simply collided here on the morning of July 1st. What happened here is incredibly rapid escalation. Within a 36-hour period, you'll have 172,000 men, almost 90,000 horses, 5,700 wagons, and over 600 pieces of artillery descending on a town with a population of slightly less than 2,400 German immigrants. These people in Gettysburg never knew what hit them. In fact, they're still trying to figure it out to this very day!

Proceeding to Gettysburg initially are 2,800 Union cavalrymen under the command of a very good and gifted Union general by the name of John Buford. Buford and his cavalry arrive in Gettysburg between 11:00 and 11:30 in the morning on June 30th, the day before the battle begins. When Buford arrives in Gettysburg, he sends out his patrols west of town and north of town, because he's heard from local farmers and his own scouts that large bodies of Confederates have been seen west and north of town.

Buford has a problem. There are five roads that come into Gettysburg from the west and north. He has to patrol, or picket, all five roads. His arc of control over these roads is a little over seven miles from flank to flank (end to end). That's a lot to ask from 2,800 Union cavalry. While Buford doesn't know which road the Confederates will be coming in on, he does predict the Battle of Gettysburg. The night before the battle begins, he turns to a fellow Union officer—a gentleman by the name of Thomas Casimer Devin—and he says, "Colonel Devin, tomorrow there will be hell to pay. They'll be coming at us three-deep." And he's right.

ON CHAMBERSBURG PIKE WHERE BATTLE OPENED

The events described in this tour occurred in the
Early morning, July 1, 1863

McPherson's Ridge ❧
❧ THE BATTLE BEGINS

The first shot of the Battle of Gettysburg is fired down this road, the Chambersburg Pike, about a mile and three-quarters in front of us. A little after 7:30 in the morning on that July 1st, one lone 2nd lieutenant in the 8th Illinois Cavalry—his name was Marcellus Jones—will raise his carbine to his shoulder and squeeze off a shot at 6,500 Confederates marching down the road—in column by fours—at him. Jones doesn't hit anyone, but the battle begins from that one simple shot.

Upon hearing that shot, John Buford—realizing that the Confederates are coming en masse down that road from the west—realizes he needs help. He sends back word eight miles due south of Gettysburg to a town called Emmitsburg, Maryland, where there are 30,000 Union infantrymen (foot soldiers). They are under the command of a major general from the state of Pennsylvania by the name of John Fulton Reynolds. Buford tells Reynolds in his communiqué that he is engaged with a large body of Confederates west of town, and he needs help.

Immediately John Fulton Reynolds orders the Union soldiers closest to Gettysburg at the time—the Union 1st Corps, about 10,000 Union infantry who had spent the night only four-and-a-half miles south of Gettysburg on the Emmitsburg Road—to drop their packs, pick up their ammunition and rifles, and get up to Gettysburg as fast as they possibly can. The Union cavalry is going to try to hold on to this ground west and north of town until the Union infantry arrives from the south.

JOHN BUFORD, USA

The Union cavalry fights extremely well for two hours, but numbers do tell. Eventually the Union cavalry is pushed back to this ridgeline we're on right now—McPherson's Ridge. It's named after a farmer, Edward McPherson, who owned the land here. When Buford gets pushed back to this position, he gets off his horse (very close to where this monument stands today) and looks behind himself, and he sees what you do if you turn around—that the town of Gettysburg starts on the other side of the next ridgeline.

HENRY HETH, CSA

He realizes he can't give up any more ground, or he'll be fighting in the streets. He must make a final determined stand along this ridge and hope that he can hold long enough until the infantry supports arrive from the south. He tells his men to dismount and to fortify this ridgeline as best they can. He places half of his available forces facing west on this side of the road (the north side of the Chambersburg Pike, to our right) and up to that distant tree line and the hill to our right (Oak Hill). On the other side of the road (to your left, on the south side of the road) he places a couple of hundred dismounted cavalrymen along the fence, and he places a couple of hundred more in that wood line. Today that wood line is called Reynolds Woods, but it's also been known as McPherson's Woods and Herbst's Woods. The balance of his command Buford keeps dismounted in the open fields on the other side of those woods, reaching down to another road that comes into Gettysburg from the west called the Fairfield/Hagerstown Road. Then Buford and his men wait for the Confederates to deploy for action.

The Confederates deploy for action on that distant ridgeline three-quarters of a mile in front of us—that's Herr's Ridge. There are 6,500 Confederate infantry and 17 cannons—all under the command of a Virginia general by the name of Henry Heth. Heth looks at the Union battle line in front of him (the same line that we're standing on right now) and determines to attack at its strongest and most defendable point—the woods to your left. Since he has been fighting the cavalry for almost two hours, he realizes that he has a golden opportunity to push the Union cavalry out of its strongest position, while he has a numerical advantage to do so.

At a quarter to ten in the morning, 1,400 Tennessee and Alabama troops under James Archer are ordered forward from that distant ridgeline. James Archer has very simple orders—to march his men across open fields (a lot more open than they are today), then strike and drive out a couple of hundred dismounted Union cavalrymen.

As Archer's Brigade advances toward those woods, it is met by the fire of the Union cavalrymen who fire a few shots at the advancing Confederates and then start abandoning these positions. The Union cavalry starts withdrawing from the woods.

Confederate commander James Archer thinks he's doing a heck of a good job—that's exactly what he was sent in to do. However the Union cavalry is not withdrawing from those woods because of the Confederate pressure; they're withdrawing because they've been relieved. Coming across the open fields over your left shoulder (from the southeast, just on the other side of McPherson's Woods) are 10,000 Union infantry coming up on the run. These are the reinforcements that were called for two hours and 20 minutes earlier—now arriving on the battlefield. These men are not coming up in one huge mass of 10,000, but they are coming up in groups of 1,000, 1,200, 1,400, or 1,600 men at a time called brigades. The first brigade in this instance—the Iron Brigade—is heading straight into those woods to take on some very surprised Confederates, who do not see them coming.

At the head of these 10,000 Union soldiers is Major General John Fulton Reynolds. He grew up only 52 miles from here in Lancaster, Pennsylvania. As he's leading in these Union soldiers, the Confederates start firing upon the Union soldiers entering these woods, and a stray shot—an overshoot—hits Reynolds in the back of the head. The bullet enters his brain behind the right ear and lodges behind his left eyeball. He is dead before he hits the ground. He'll be the highest-ranking Union officer to be killed at the Battle of Gettysburg. The Union soldiers fight on, hitting the Confederates from three different directions in those woods—from the front, from the flank (side of the line), and even from the Confederate rear—eventually causing 350 casualties in the Confederate column. The Union soldiers drive the Confederates back into those woods, to a position in the northwestern corner of McPherson's Woods, to a place called Willoughby Run. That's where the demise of Archer's Brigade takes place.

JOHN F. REYNOLDS, USA

WILLOUGHBY RUN, SHOWING 19TH INDIANA MONUMENT

The events described in this tour occurred in the
Morning, July 1, 1863

Willoughby Run

GENERAL ARCHER'S CONFEDERATES MEET THE IRON BRIGADE

Now we're at Willoughby Run. The Confederates—James Archer's brigade that first advanced against the dismounted Union cavalry—are coming in from the west (in front of us), over open fields. They've been taking fire from the dismounted Union cavalry, but as they cross the creek here, they start driving the Union cavalry back. Well, the Union cavalry is withdrawing, not because of Confederate pressure, but because the Union infantry has now arrived on the field.

JAMES J. ARCHER, CSA

The infantry that hits Archer's Brigade in these woods is one of the finest outfits in the entire Union army—mid-westerners from the states of Michigan, Wisconsin, and Indiana, known as the Iron Brigade. They earned their nickname, Iron Brigade, for their reputation of never taking a step back in battle during two years of fighting. That's quite a reputation for any Union group in 1863! They hit Archer's Brigade in the middle of these woods from their front (Archer's right flank), and to some extent, they penetrate Archer's rear. They drive Archer's Brigade back through these woods—a running battle of almost 700 yards, to the position we're standing on right now.

The 1st Tennessee and the 14th Tennessee are bottled up in this creek bed, using the creek bed as a line of defense, when Union soldiers again come over the high ground, through these woods from the east. More Union soldiers straddle the creek bed and come in from the south, and some Union soldiers get into the open fields beyond, to swing in behind Archer's Brigade.

What drives Archer's capture, and the capture of many of his men, is the 2nd Wisconsin—the unit that led the charge of the Iron Brigade into these woods. When the men get on the high ground directly above this creek, Company B—the right-most company of the 2nd Wisconsin—extends its lines to your right and takes position on the high ground above this quarry, which was here at the time of the battle. Many members of Company B continue down, gaining the creek and coming in on the Confederate left flank. On the other side of the creek, about 35 paces away from the bend in the creek—which we're standing at right now—is the site where James Archer and a number of his officers are captured.

This is the demise of Archer's Brigade. When the counting is over that day, Archer has lost 350 men—killed, wounded and captured—on this position. The Iron Brigade as a whole suffered against Archer's Brigade that day, but the 2nd Wisconsin Infantry suffered the largest toll. The Wisconsin men led the charge into these woods and pushed Archer's Brigade back into this position—a move that was probably most responsible for Archer's capture. The 2nd Wisconsin lost nearly 77% of its men that day—most against Archer's Brigade in the morning fight here at Willoughby Run.

WILLOUGHBY RUN

THE RAILROAD CUT

The events described in this tour occurred in the
Morning, July 1, 1863

The Railroad Cut ❧

THE FIGHT FOR THE COLORS OF THE SECOND MISSISSIPPI

We're in the Railroad Cut. There are 10,000 Union soldiers coming up from the Emmitsburg, Maryland area, arriving from the south and the southeast (through these fields front of us). First the Iron Brigade advances diagonally across these fields and into the woods, very close to the spot where General Reynolds is killed.

That morning attack by the Confederates was not limited to James Archer's brigade advancing against the dismounted Union cavalry along McPherson's Ridge, for there was also action north of the Chambersburg Pike in this area. Brigadier General Joseph Davis' brigade, about 1,700 men (three regiments), advanced at the same time that Archer's Brigade moved against the dismounted cavalry in those woods to our left. Davis' Brigade swung wide, coming in here to your right (the ridgeline in front of us). That gentleman on the pedestal is Major General James Wadsworth, and he is actually pointing at the middle of Joseph Davis' brigade advancing at him from the north.

As more and more of these Union soldiers arrive from the south, they throw themselves into the positions previously held by the Union cavalry along McPherson's Ridge. As these Union soldiers advance into these open fields, they cross right near us and swing across this field to the top of the ridgeline there. The two regiments at the right end of the line are the 56th Pennsylvania (the monument with the crossed muskets) and the 76th New York. These two regiments swing up, trying to prolong the same line that the

JOSEPH R. DAVIS, CSA

JAMES S. WADSWORTH, USA

Union cavalry had before them. Unfortunately, as they go up and over the rise, as James Wadsworth is indicating, they meet Joseph Davis' brigade, only a couple of hundred yards away.

At this point, these two Union regiments are at the mercy of the Confederates. The 55th North Carolina (the extreme left of Davis' Brigade) hits the 76th New York in flank and threatens its rear. The 76th New York and the 56th Pennsylvania break, and they retreat across these open fields with the Confederates in tow. These two Union regiments retreat across the open fields to the high ground on our right rear—the Railroad Woods. The woods were not as thick as they are today (it was open ground), and those two Union regiments make a stand there. They rally and, in fact, start firing back at Joe Davis' brigade advancing again toward them.

Davis, however, has another problem. More and more Union soldiers are coming up—including a couple of Union regiments held in reserve. One of those regiments is the 6th Wisconsin Infantry, a portion of the Iron Brigade that has been held out of the fight in those woods against James Archer's Brigade. They had been at the Lutheran Seminary.

With the death of John Fulton Reynolds, Major General Abner Doubleday is now in command, and he sees the Confederate successes here. On his right flank—the Union 1st Corps—the Union infantry is deploying, and he sends over those regiments to take a position along that road right there (the Chambersburg Pike, which had fences along the road). Doubleday places the 6th Wisconsin directly in front of us. To their left (about where the ridgeline is), he places the 95th New York and, to their left, the 84th New York (more commonly know as the 14th Brooklyn).

The Union advance against this position is done in echelon—a term which indicates a wave attack, like a wave breaking upon a beach. If you've ever seen a wave breaking on a beach, a part of it breaks, then another part breaks, then another part. That's exactly the way the Union soldiers attack the Railroad Cut. The 6th Wisconsin charges first, then a couple minutes later, the 95th New York charge to their left, and then a few minutes later, the 84th New York (the 14th Brooklyn) charges.

The 2nd Mississippi is in the position we are standing on right now. The soldiers of the 55th North Carolina, to our left, are taking care of the Union soldiers they've routed back to the high ground in the Railroad Woods. Suddenly Joseph Davis realizes he is in a predicament—there are 1,320 Union soldiers directly in front of him—and he decides to call for a retreat. He wants to withdraw as best he can.

The orders that he gives are somewhat nebulous, so many of his men just step out of the low part of the cut where we're standing, and they retreat the same way they came in. However, many unsuspecting Confederates begin withdrawing up the railroad bed to Herr's Ridge, which is about a mile beyond the Railroad Cut Bridge. Unfortunately, with every step they take to the right—or up the railroad bed toward Herr's Ridge, retreating back to the west—they are getting into worse ground, increasingly high ground. Colonel Dawes of the 6th Wisconsin—the first Union regiment to charge across these fields—tells his men not to fire a shot until they reach the cut so that they will have loaded weapons to fire down at the helpless Confederates. Then the 95th New York and the 84th New York hit them in subsequent blows. When it is all over, there are about 49 dead Confederates counted in the cut, with 233 captured, mostly from the 2nd Mississippi and the 55th North Carolina in the deeper part of the cut.

RUFUS R. DAWES, USA

88—Oak Hill—from Observatory.

OAK HILL FROM OBSERVATORY

The events described in this tour occurred in the
Midday, July 1, 1863

Oak Hill

CONFEDERATE REINFORCEMENTS ARRIVE FROM THE NORTH

The first day at Gettysburg is a remarkable day to study because you're never quite sure where your opponent will be coming from. It's a day of concentration, so it's a day of surprises. The Union army is on three different roads coming in from two different directions—from the south, which you're facing, and from the southeast. The Confederate army is on four different roads coming in from three different directions that day, initially from the west—the Confederates we've been talking about up to this point. Henry Heth's division arrives on the Chambersburg Pike, coming from the west.

But at 12 o'clock in the afternoon, the next threat to the Union army comes from the north, when 8,000 Confederates step out of the tree line behind us. This is Major General Robert Rodes' Confederate division. Still later in the day, about a mile to our left, coming in from the northeast will be Major General Jubal Early's division. We'll be discussing them a little bit later.

The Union position, at about 12 o'clock in the afternoon, starts in those woods in front of us (McPherson's Woods), where the Iron Brigade fought Archer's Brigade in the morning. That's McPherson's barn, that brick and white structure. As the Union soldiers arrive that day, they deploy along the ridgeline that you see directly in front of us (McPherson's Ridge). However, they're not able to extend their line as far as the Union cavalry had done before them, because of the advance of Robert Rodes' Confederate division from the north. In fact, the Union battle line extends only up to that first line of trees, mid-way between our position and McPherson's barn in the distance.

ROBERT E. RODES, CSA

This is a very good position to see where the Confederates arrive from the west (Archer and Davis' brigades). Throughout the day, they assemble and advance from that ridgeline—Herr's Ridge, where you see the red and blue barn, the white silo, and the white houses along the ridgeline.

When 8,000 Confederates come in behind us, Robert Rodes finds himself in a remarkably good situation. He is on the flank of the Union position—like a big "T," about as good as you can get, tactically speaking, in the American Civil War. This position is a general's heaven, and Rodes has to be salivating at the prospect here. The very first thing he does is set up 14 cannons on top of this hill, to start firing down the Union battle line. From that fire, about 500 Union soldiers retreat from McPherson's Ridge across these open fields and into that tree line—the Railroad Woods again. Rodes sees those men retreating into the woods, and he is determined to go after them. He tells Brigadier General Alfred Iverson to take his 1,400 North Carolinians off this hill, with the idea of driving out those 500 or so Union soldiers in the woods.

Unfortunately he tells the wrong man to do the job. Whether Alfred Iverson was drunk, scared or stupid, he would not lead his men into battle. He yells out, "Give 'em hell, boys!" but he does not go with them. Those 1,400 North Carolinians enter this fight, advancing across these open fields, with the idea of driving out the 500 or so Union soldiers in the woods. Unfortunately, an absentee general is the least of their problems. On our left there, on the other side of the tree line, is a valley. In fact, what we're looking at (to your left and left front) is the ridgeline called Oak Ridge. There is a three-and-a-half foot stone wall—a former boundary wall—that starts in those woods and goes down to that road—the Mummasburg Road.

ALFRED IVERSON, CSA

What these Confederates don't realize is that 3,000 more Union soldiers have come up from the southeast (we're facing southeast). They have used the ridgeline and the tree line to place themselves behind that former boundary wall. Now the Confederates are expecting to find 500 Union soldiers in the tree line, but they are not expecting to find 3,000 Union soldiers directly in front of them. Those Union soldiers hold their fire until the Confederates are just 80 yards away.

When the Confederates get to within 80 yards, the Union commanders give the order to "up, and fire." Three thousand Union soldiers stand up, level their rifles, and fire a volley right into the faces of the North Carolinians. They never saw it coming. Five hundred more Union soldiers in the tree line in the Railroad Woods open up on their flank. These Confederates go down by the hundreds in the first volley. Here at Gettysburg we call it Iverson's Massacre, or the North Carolina Sacrifice. One Confederate account places the number as high as 500 men falling in the first volley. If that's true, it's remarkable. There was one North Carolina corporal buried later that afternoon with six separate bullet holes in his head alone. All the Confederates can do is go to ground in the lowest depression—the only thing they had. This was a timothy field then—high grass for horses, but only ankle deep at the time of the battle. The Confederates remain in that precarious position for almost 35 minutes. Finally seeing a helpless enemy less than 100 yards away, the Union commanders order their men to fix bayonets and charge. To make a long story short of a very bloody affair, Iverson's Brigade suffers the highest percentage of loss of any Confederate brigade at the entire Battle of Gettysburg, and they never saw it coming.

This is another Union success on July 1st. Later in the day, however, Robert Rodes is successful in driving the Union soldiers from that position when he attacks from three different directions in a coordinated manner. Rodes leads 7,000 Confederate troops, having lost the thousand now lying in front of that wall.

STEPHEN D. RAMSEUR, CSA

More North Carolinians under the youngest general in the Confederate army, Stephen Dodson Ramseur, come swinging in right over the dead bodies of Iverson's men. Alabamans straddle this ridgeline and work their way to the Union flank, which is the confluence of that road and the tree line. Georgia and Alabama troops coming from the valley beyond (to our left), swing up and attack the Union position from behind, cutting off the retreat of the Union soldiers from the ridgeline, ultimately producing a 67% loss to the Union outfits that remain. What I have described here is called the Battle of Oak Ridge—one of the bloodiest affairs at Gettysburg. In approximately three hours—from 1 o'clock until 4 o'clock in the afternoon—there are 4,200 American casualties, with one in every three a fatality. That figure is the highest mortality rate on the battle-field, and most of those are from Iverson's Brigade, taking it clean in the teeth at 80 yards.

Eventually, more Confederates arrive from a different road, coming in from the northeast (that's well to our left), and we'll be heading in that direction next. The Union battle line breaks down from right to left, and it starts on a little knoll of ground that we call Barlow's Knoll.

TREE LINE AND FIELD OF IVERSON'S MASSACRE

BARLOW'S KNOLL FROM ROCK CREEK

The events described in this tour occurred in the
Afternoon, July 1, 1863

Barlow's Knoll
UNION LINE BREAKS DOWN FROM RIGHT TO LEFT

Now we are on the Union right flank. We just came from Oak Ridge (the distant tree line), where Iverson's men were slaughtered in the fields (on the other side of that ridgeline). That's where those 3,000 Union soldiers in Iverson's front and 500 more Union soldiers on his flank absolutely devastated that North Carolina brigade. After the Confederates go to ground, several thousand more Union soldiers arrive from town. They take positions north of town, in these open fields—very poor positions. What we're standing on right now is the Union right flank, at a place called Barlow's Knoll. It was called Blocher's Knoll at the time of the battle because it was named after the farmer who owned the property. It was renamed Barlow's Knoll for the Union general, Frances Barlow, whose men fought and bled on this ground.

FRANCES BARLOW, USA

As I said earlier, the 1st of July is a remarkable day to study because you're never quite sure where your opponent will be coming from. Initially the Confederates arrive from the west. Later Robert Rodes' division arrives from the north. Then at about 2 o'clock in the afternoon, coming down a road on the other side of that tree line to your front-right are 6,000 Confederates under the command of Major General Jubal Early.

The first attack by Jubal Early is with nine regiments from the state of Georgia, under the command of John B. Gordon. They hit the Union position here and completely envelop the knoll itself. Also coming down the road are 2,550 Louisiana and North Carolina

JUBAL A. EARLY, CSA

troops that are threatening, not only the flank, but also swinging into the rear of the Union position in the open valleys behind us.

The Union battle line is being subjected to an awful lot of gunfire. In fact, the men of the 153rd Pennsylvania (this monument right here) said they only fired their weapons about five times before they were forced to withdraw. There are about 200 men down on the military crest of this hill. The 153rd Pennsylvania is drawn up in two ranks, one rank right behind the other. However, they only fire their weapons a few times before they are beaten back by the 38th and the 61st Georgia from John B. Gordon's brigade. As they start to withdraw, the Union right flank begins to crumble.

Down near the cemetery (that's the Alms House Cemetery) there's a Union general by the name of Adelbert Ames. Ames sees his Union right flank breaking under the pressure of these Georgia outfits, so he sends forward the seven companies of Lieutenant Colonel Douglas Fowler's 17th Connecticut Volunteers. Fowler is told to pull his sword and lead his men forward to stabilize things on Ames' right flank, as the 153rd Pennsylvania is withdrawing. These guns right behind us are Bayard Wilkeson's guns. There were four guns here, battling 14 guns a half-mile away, that had come in with Jubal Early. Early's artillery is firing over his own men, firing and exploding case shot in this area. Douglas Fowler, colonel of the 17th Connecticut, moves forward into position, trying to stabilize the Union right flank, when a Confederate case shot explodes right in front of his face, decapitating him and spraying blood and brain matter all over the men of the 17th Connecticut. It was later recorded by the 153rd Pennsylvania troops, who were retreating through the ranks of the 17th Connecticut, that when the Fowler's head exploded, his men (the 17th Connecticut) turned green, dropped their weapons, and headed for the rear.

DOUGLAS FOWLER, USA

Now the entire Union battle line breaks down from right to left. The retreat then spreads to Oak Ridge. As far away as McPherson's Ridge, the retreat grows, with the Union Iron Brigade (the first Union outfit we discussed) withdrawing from those woods and moving to the Lutheran Seminary, where they make a final stand before they are forced to withdraw back through the streets of Gettysburg to Cemetery Hill.

The turn of events started here on Blocher's Knoll, or Barlow's Knoll—the entire Union battle line breaking down because one lieutenant colonel lost his head in battle!

ROCK CREEK

THE THOMPSON HOUSE—GENERAL ROBERT E. LEE'S HEADQUARTERS

The events described in this tour occurred in the
Afternoon, July 1, 1863

Seminary Ridge

UNION FIRST CORPS MAKES FINAL STAND BEFORE RETREATING THROUGH TOWN

We're now on Seminary Ridge, on the far left of the Union battle line. That battle line is breaking down on July 1st from right to left. The positions in front of you are the last to break, with Union soldiers making a final stand among the buildings behind us (the Lutheran Seminary), before their lines again break and they are driven through the streets of Gettysburg.

What you see here, you've seen before. That group of woods directly in front of us is where General Reynolds was killed while leading in the Iron Brigade against General Archer's brigade about 10 o'clock in the morning. The Iron Brigade drove Archer's Brigade almost 700 yards down to the northwestern corner of those woods to Willoughby Run, where Archer was captured and his brigade suffered 350 casualties.

JAMES J. PETTIGREW, CSA

The Union soldiers (the Iron Brigade) who were successful against Archer's Brigade are told to hold on to those woods throughout the day. About 2 o'clock in the afternoon, the Confederates advance from Herr's Ridge (that distant tree line about a mile and a half in front of us). More Confederates—a large brigade of 2,600 men under the command of General James Pettigrew—advance and attack the Iron Brigade in those woods yet again. At 2 o'clock in the afternoon, they close to within 60 feet of the Union position and fight the Iron Brigade for nearly two hours. They drive the Union soldiers out of the woods, back to these positions, just slightly left of where we're standing now. Thousands more Union soldiers throughout the day will also retreat back to these positions.

DORSEY PENDER, CSA

If you look to your right, you can see a ridgeline with monuments. That's the Railroad Cut, which we discussed earlier in the fight. The Union soldiers along that ridgeline and on the one just directly in front, also withdraw back to this position as more and more Confederates enter the fight. Heth's Division has been fighting most of the day, with mixed results. Earlier in the day, the Confederates lost their fight in those woods when Archer was pushed out by the Iron Brigade. They also lost at the Railroad Cut when Joe Davis' brigade was pushed out of that position. They are successful, however, when Pettigrew's Brigade breaks the Union position in those woods (McPherson's Woods). They drive the Union soldiers back to these positions.

The Union cannons that had been in these positions forward of us had battled the Confederates arriving from the west and north. Those cannons have now also withdrawn to this position, and they make a final stand here. There are 21 Union cannons—17 of them north of the Seminary building (just over our left shoulder). The right of the artillery line is just to the right of the Chambersburg Pike, firing down toward the Confederates who are coming up and over that high ground, very close to the Railroad Cut Bridge.

The Union soldiers stand here as long as they possibly can, but more Confederates are now entering the fight. Major General Dorsey Pender's Confederate division takes over the assault from the Confederates attacking from the west. Thousands more Confederates now advance from the west—right over the prone bodies of many of Heth's Division, that has now gone to ground at that first ridgeline directly in front of us.

Two brigades cause the most problems for the Union troops along Seminary Ridge—their last stand facing west before their lines are broken and they are driven through the streets of Gettysburg. Scales' North Carolina brigade comes over that rise in front of us, the left flank straddling the road. Then Perrin's Brigade of South Carolinians comes in on our left.

Let's examine Scales' Brigade first. The left-most regiment is the 38th North Carolina. These men straddle the road as they advance toward us. To their right is the unlucky 13th North Carolina. These men advance down the road (toward these positions), and the rest of Scales' Brigade continues to their right. Further to their right is Perrin's Brigade. As they come down the slope and head into this field, Scales' Brigade is being hit, not only by thousands of Union infantry still fighting along this ridgeline, but by at least 17 cannons. In fact, Scales' Brigade will go down as a result of this artillery fire.

Let's talk about canister. Canister is a tin can that holds anywhere from 26 to 30 one-inch iron balls packed with sawdust, and when you ram them down the muzzle of any cannon with two-and-a-half pounds of gunpowder and ignite the gunpowder, the canister ruptures in the muzzle, and you have 26 to 30 one-inch iron balls flying at you. They say one of these balls can cut a man in half at 500 yards. Well, as Scales' left flank comes up and over that ridgeline, the men take enormous canister fire from the Union artillery directly in their front and slightly off their flank (just across the Chambersburg Pike). In fact, they are stopped almost completely by the canister fire. Nathan Smith, an adjutant from the 13th North Carolina, recalled that when the regiment got to within 75 yards of the enemy position, the men were ordered to lie down. Of the 180 men in the regiment, 150 were killed or wounded, leaving only 30 men commanded by just two officers. Of the 38th North Carolina, which straddles the road, 130 men are killed and wounded (out of 216), probably from the canister fire from the right flank of the last position held by the Union here on July 1st.

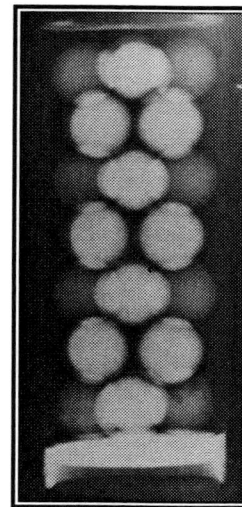

CANISTER

There are 17 cannon holding back Scales' North Carolinians. In fact, halfway between our position and that first ridgeline in front of you is where Scales goes to ground. Perrin's South Carolinians, however, do not have that same artillery fire to deal with. There are only four cannons firing at Perrin's Brigade as they advance against what's left of the Union Iron Brigade, which has backed up and taken the position just to our left. Off their left flank is where Perrin's Brigade will actually break the Union position. The 1st and 14th

South Carolina swing around, break the Union position (just off the left flank of the Iron Brigade) and start heading in this direction (north), trying to grab as many Union cannons as they possibly can. It's now the job of the Union infantry to hold Scales' Brigade in front and Perrin's Brigade on their flank. The Union infantry wants to hold long enough until their 21 cannons can limber up and enable the men to retreat through the streets of Gettysburg to the predetermined fallback point south of town—Cemetery Hill. They are successful in a fight that lasts about 20 minutes. It's an ugly little fight, with Union soldiers holding as long as they possibly can, saving their own artillery by their sacrifice along this ridgeline.

After this ridgeline is cleared of all Union resistance, Robert E. Lee (who had reached this battlefield about 12 o'clock in the afternoon) advances his headquarters forward. Eventually he pitches his headquarters tents in the fields just to our right (that monument indicates his headquarters position). When his men are tenting, Lee is usually tenting, as well. He pitches his command tents in this area just to our right. He may also have used that stone building (Thompson House) as a part of his headquarters, taking a few meals there; but he commands from this general area during the remaining portion of the Battle of Gettysburg. He may also have used the Seminary cupola for part of his observation, looking at the Union build-up south of town on July 2nd and 3rd.

SEMINARY RIDGE NORTH TO OAK RIDGE

THE EVERGREEN CEMETERY GATEHOUSE FROM CEMETERY HILL

The events described in this tour occurred in the
Evening, July 1, 1863

Cemetery Hill

UNION TROOPS REORGANIZE ON HIGH GROUND SOUTH OF TOWN

Where we are now is Cemetery Hill. This is the rallying point for the Union soldiers after the defeat on July 1st. The Seminary is just off to your left front on the other side of town. The last stand of the Union soldier on that July 1st is at the Seminary. Confederates drive the Union soldiers back through the streets of Gettysburg to join their fellow soldiers who have retreated from the north. The retreat through town is a miserable affair for the Union army. The Confederates are no more than 300 yards away at any one point, and as a result, there are almost 3,000 killed, wounded, and captured Union soldiers in the streets of Gettysburg before they arrive at this position. This was predetermined—this spot that we're standing on right now. As soon as John Buford, leading his cavalry, knew that this good ground south of town existed,—he selected it as the rallying point of the Union army.

OLIVER O. HOWARD, USA

Much of the command on July 1st is from this hill. Many Union generals, including Oliver Otis Howard who led the Union 11th Corps which had fought north of town, later commanded from this hill, where one could overlook the town and see the fields west and north of it. When the Union soldiers break and retreat to this position, they fall in with many other Union soldiers who have been coming here throughout the day. As more and more Union soldiers arrive at this position that day, the Union generals are no longer willing to throw good men into a bad situation west and north of town. Instead they keep Union brigades up here digging entrenchments and fortifying artillery positions so that when their lines finally do break west and north of town, they can rally back into strength.

There is a bit of a command problem that day. John Fulton Reynolds certainly would have commanded the entire day, had he not been killed so early in the fight. His successor, Abner Doubleday, has a confrontation with Oliver Otis Howard as to who is in command. Finally, a stabilizing influence arrives on the battlefield—Major General Winfield Scott Hancock. Hancock has been sent here by Meade with written orders to take control of the situation here at Gettysburg. Now Hancock sizes up this position, and he settles down the retreating Union soldiers, placing them into battle line, thus making it almost impossible for the Confederates to continue their advance against this position.

WINFIELD S. HANCOCK, USA

It has been said, by most Southerners anyway, that there was a discretionary order given to Richard Ewell, a major general commanding one-third of Lee's army here at Gettysburg. It is Ewell's men—Robert Rodes' command and Jubal Early's command—who come in from the north and the northeast that day. Ewell is given a discretionary order to continue the attack that late afternoon and early evening on Cemetery Hill, *if practicable*. Ewell decides that it is not practicable, and I believe he was probably right *not* to attack. This is sometimes called the Stonewall Jackson Scenario: if Jackson had not been killed two months earlier at the Battle of Chancellorsville, and if Jackson had been given that same order (to attack this hill, if practicable), he certainly would have attacked.

I'm not so sure Jackson would have been successful, however. The reason is that there comes a time when the Union generals here are no longer willing to throw good men into a bad situation. They have an awful lot of Union soldiers digging in on this hill. In addition, the Union soldiers retiring from those fields west and north of town are digging in alongside them.

RICHARD S. EWELL, CSA

The battle line is getting stronger and stronger every moment. More Union soldiers are coming up the Baltimore Pike and they are being deployed in and around this area. As the Confederates enter the town following the Union retreat, the continuity of the battle lines breaks, as well. The only way Ewell has any chance of success in continuing the attack on Cemetery Hill is to extricate his troops from town, place them on either side of the hill, and then attack this hill in a coordinated manner. I personally don't believe there was a window of opportunity for Ewell to have done that. Every moment you give the Union position here, it is getting stronger and stronger. I don't believe the Confederates could have succeeded in driving the Union from this hill that day—especially after Hancock arrived.

Then Hancock places his troops in a position that will eventually form the shape of a hook—now called the "fish-hook." He places Union soldiers on the night of July 1st on that hill—that's Culp's Hill. The line continues through this hill, and then makes an abrupt left-hand turn through the cemetery on our left, to a hill about two-and-a-half miles south of town, called Little Round Top. This fishhook defines the ground on which the Union army will eventually win the Battle of Gettysburg.

The first day is a remarkable day of sacrifice. The Union soldiers sacrifice themselves to gain time for the army to arrive and secure these positions south of town. Of the 15,000 Union soldiers who fight on July 1st, nearly 9,000 are killed, wounded or captured. Of the 29,600 Confederates who fight here on July 1st, almost 6,000 are killed, wounded or captured. The first day at Gettysburg, there are almost 15,000 casualties, which make it no small affair.

Even though the Union army lost that day's fight, it gained the ground that it would fight on during the next two days. In fact, when Lee attacks the next day—July 2nd—there are 80,000 Union soldiers on a three-mile-long line in the shape of a fishhook.

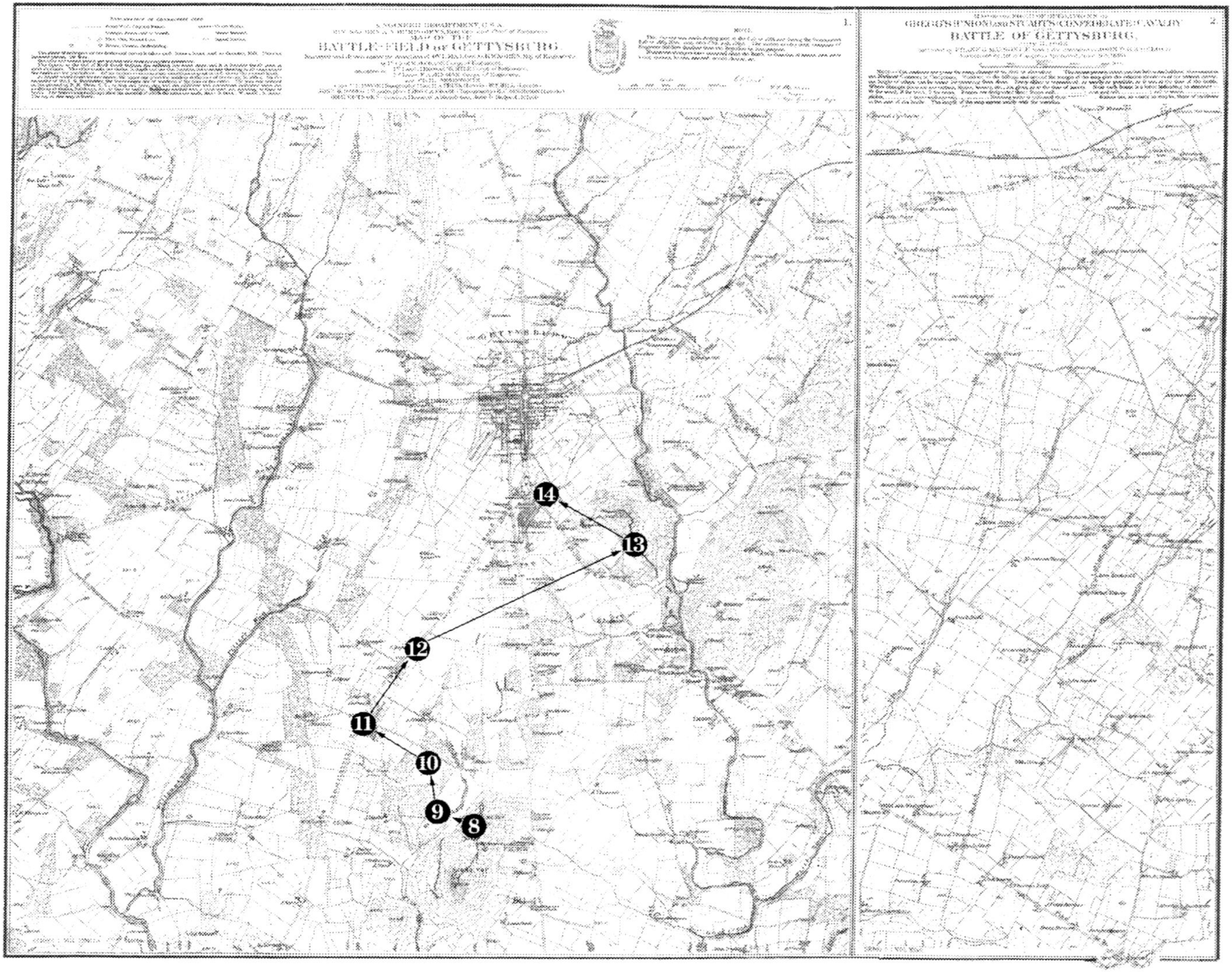

MAP OF THE
BATTLE-FIELD of GETTYSBURG
1.
BATTLE OF GETTYSBURG,
2.
8
9
10
11
12
13
14

Audio 2 Tour

LITTLE ROUND TOP TOWARDS DEVIL'S DEN

The events described in this tour occurred in the
Afternoon, July 2, 1863

Little Round Top ∽

CONFEDERATE ATTACK ON UNION LEFT REPULSED AT THE POINT OF A BAYONET

We're at Little Round Top now. This is the left flank of the Union "fishhook" line. The Union battle line starts just short of this hill and goes in that direction, past that dome memorial (the Pennsylvania Memorial), up to that white building (a park building called the Cyclorama), and from there it abruptly turns to the right. So there's your fishhook—it goes down and then hooks to the right.

The Confederate battle line is the tree line past the last green fields that you see in the distance, and it continues all the way until it disappears behind the high ground on our left (Big Round Top). Now there are 10,000 Union soldiers in the battle line, from the Pennsylvania Memorial to just short of this hill. Those solders are under the command of a political general from the state of New York by the name of Daniel Sickles. As soon as Sickles is placed on the Union left flank in that position, he doesn't like it. The reason he doesn't like it is that he's been given the only low ground on the entire Union battle line to defend, and it's no fun to defend low ground in any war. On his own and without orders, he breaks away from the rest of the Union battle line and advances his men forward, looking for better positions. Now he's putting the entire Union battle line at great risk because he is moving forward up to three-quarters of a mile. Now again, he should have been in a straight line from that dome memorial to, and including, this hill and the Union defenses. Those were his orders. Instead he moves forward of it. If you look out there you'll see two red barns way in the distance, along the Emmitsburg Road. That's how far Sickles moves without orders. His battle line starts to the right of the last red barn, and it continues to the left,

DANIEL E. SICKLES, USA

past both red barns, to a place called The Peach Orchard. At that point, his line bends back through these trees somewhat toward us, up and over that ridgeline in front of us, and he places his left flank in those rocks (Devil's Den). So you can see, Sickles is not where he's supposed to be. I mean, big time, he is not supposed to be out there.

When George Gordon Meade, the Union commander, finds out about this, he is furious. He goes looking for Sickles. And he finds Sickles up near the Peach Orchard, about three-quarters of a mile from this hill, at about 3:20 in the afternoon on that July 2nd. When he finds him, Meade says, "Sickles, what have you done?" Sickles very calmly replies, "Well sir, I thought I could adjust my battle lines." Meade very sarcastically says, "Yes, General, but I didn't expect a general advance upon Richmond." Sickles, sensing the sarcasm and anger in Meade's voice, suggests maybe he pull back to where he should have been—back to this hill, and back to the low ground of the "fishhook", reconnecting with the rest of the Union army. Before he can give those orders, however, 54 Confederate cannons from that distant tree line start firing at Sickles' lines. That's when 23,000 Confederates begin their assault upon Sickles' lines. It's too late. The only thing that George Gordon Meade, the Union commander, can do is send reinforcements out to Sickles and hope for the best.

GOUVERNEUR K. WARREN, USA

On this portion of the battlefield, not the commanding general has decided where to fight, but an insubordinate political general from the state of New York—Dan Sickles—who chooses to place his command three-quarters of a mile in front of the rest of the Union army. It's no wonder that George Gordon Meade now loses all faith in Dan Sickles; so he sends a man to this portion of the battlefield, a man he feels he can trust. He sends that man—Brigadier General Gouverneur Kemble Warren, Chief Engineer of the Union army. Warren is sent here by Meade to ascertain exactly how strong Sickles' new lines are and where the reinforcements should be sent. Those lines out there are now being attacked, so he does what we do—he comes to this high ground to get a better view. He and his aides come riding up to this hill. As they ascend this hill, to their horror, they realize that Dan Sickles has left this hill unoccupied. There's nobody up here. Now Warren gets very anxious about this. He climbs off his horse and climbs up on that rock. If you were to do the same thing and look over his shoulder, what you would see is a distant field well to our left. What he sees coming out of that tree line is a force of 1,850 Alabama and Texas Confederates. They're not heading for any portion of Dan Sickles' lines, however. Instead, they're going around them. They're going to go up and over Big Round Top (the hill on our left), and they're going to try to take this hill. If they take it, where will they be? They'll be behind a portion of the Union army, on high ground on the flank of the rest of the Union army.

Warren and his staff know they have to do something. They get on their horses, and they go looking for Union soldiers. About half a mile to your right (closer to the "fishhook"), they find 1,450 Union soldiers under the command of a colonel by the name of Strong Vincent. One of Warren's staff members points up to this hill and says, "Colonel Vincent, do you see yonder hill?" Vincent acknowledges that he does, and he is told to get his command up here as fast as he possibly can. It is now a race between those 1,450 Union soldiers and those 1,850 Alabama and Texas Confederates, and whoever wins that race, has the key position on the entire battlefield of Gettysburg. This hill commands one half of the entire Union battle line.

STRONG VINCENT, USA

Well, the Union soldiers win the race to this hill by five minutes. The battle is fought half-way up the southern and southwestern slopes of the hill on this little ledge that you see to our left (you see a monument, an evergreen tree, another monument, an evergreen tree, and then two other monuments further to the left of that evergreen tree on the southern slope of the hill). Union soldiers take position along that ledge, which we call Vincent's Spur today. They are in position only five minutes when the Confederates attack. The Confederate attack will eventually spread around both Union flanks on the hill. The first flank they attack is the Union left flank. In that direction about 150 yards from here, 377 men from the state of Maine—the 20th Maine Volunteer Infantry—under the command of a colonel by the name of Joshua Lawrence Chamberlain, a school teacher by trade, are attacked by 650 Alabamans—the 15th and 47th Alabama Infantry.

JOSHUA L. CHAMBERLAIN, USA

It is one of the most severe fights of the American Civil War, certainly one of the most severe fights here at Gettysburg. In 50 minutes, it goes to hand-to-hand fighting five separate times. The fight degenerates to men throwing rocks at each other. Finally, when the Union commander, Chamberlain, realizes his men are out of ammunition, and he sees no support coming up for him, he gives the only command he feels he can give, "Bayonet, bayonet, forward!" Two hundred men—that's all he could spare for the attack—affix bayonets and charge an overwhelming number of Alabamans, and they are successful. At the point of a bayonet, they drive those Alabamans off that flank, to secure that flank. And for that bayonet charge, Colonel Joshua Lawrence Chamberlain will be awarded the Congressional Medal of Honor (by the way, one of 61 that are issued to Union soldiers at the Battle of Gettysburg).

However, this hill is secured not by one bayonet charge but by two. To your left (between these two evergreen trees along that ledge), there are about 200 men from the state of Michigan—the 16th Michigan Volunteer Infantry. They are beaten back by the repeated attacks of 800 Texas Confederates—the 4th and 5th Texas Infantry. When the Texans prevail and gain access to that ledge, they start pushing the Union flank up toward the top of the hill. Things do not look good for the Union cause at Gettysburg because the Union right flank on Little Round Top has been turned. Fortunately for the Union cause, General Warren has not been sitting idly by. While all this is going on, he has been down in those valleys to your right looking for as many Union soldiers as he can possibly redirect to this hill; and those Union soldiers begin to arrive.

WILLIAM C. OATES, CSA

The first to arrive are 535 New Yorkers—the 140th New York Infantry—under the command of Colonel Patrick Henry O'Rorke, who graduated first in his class at West Point in June of 1861 (the same class in which George Armstrong Custer graduated last). Now O'Rorke has been told personally by Warren to get his command to this hill and waste no time about it. He's issued no orders for his men to load weapons. Since these are muzzle-loading rifles, it takes 20, 30, sometimes 35 seconds to load a weapon in those days. He isn't going to take the time because he's going to get his men to the hill, and then they'll worry about loading. Well, when he comes up and over the crest of the hill (where these monuments are on our left, and where that castle monument is on our left), he looks forward, and what does he see just in yards ahead of him? He sees hundreds of Texans looking back at him. There's still no time to load weapons, so the only command O'Rorke can give is, "Fix bayonets!" Five hundred and thirty-five New Yorkers prepare to fight with fixed bayonets. Paddy O'Rorke draws his sword, and with the words, "Down this way, boys!" he leads them in a desperate bayonet charge against hundreds of Texans now returning fire. In a matter of minutes, almost a third of the New Yorkers are shot down, including their colonel. O'Rorke is shot through the throat, and he bleeds to death on this hill, but the New Yorkers do not stop. They're now all over the Texans, and, at the point of a bayonet, they drive the Texans off the slope to secure the flank on the hill.

PATRICK H. O'RORKE, USA

You know, the bayonet was not an overly used weapon in the American Civil War. Most soldiers used them for tent pegs and candleholders. Yet in the most important battle ever fought on the North American continent, both Union flanks are secured by desperate Union bayonet charges. These movements make Little Round Top one of the most studied military actions in the entire world.

LARGE BOULDERS AT DEVIL'S DEN

The events described in this tour occurred in the
Afternoon, July 2, 1863

Devil's Den

FIGHTING INTENSIFIES AS COMBAT GOES HAND TO HAND AMONGST THE ROCKS

You're at Devil's Den. This is the left flank of Dan Sickles' line. Remember, he has pushed forward, away from the "fishhook" line and he anchors his left flank in these rocks. He has about 1,500 Union soldiers in these rocks, on top of these rocks, and down along the ridgeline to our right. This ridgeline exits into a place called The Wheatfield, well to our right. Sickles has four cannons up here, as well. It's a pretty strong position, as you can see. However, the Confederates eventually compromise this position by totally encircling it and forcing the Union soldiers to withdraw.

Now if you want to pan around to your left, you'll see Big Round Top and Little Round Top. The Confederates are attacking Little Round Top. In fact, they'll be attacking Little Round Top and Devil's Den almost at the same time. As a result, you'll have Confederates who are going up and over Big Round Top to attack the Union position on Little Round Top. Other Confederates attack this position, as well. As I mentioned earlier, the first Confederate attack comes from the west.

AUGUSTUS V. H. ELLIS, USA

These guns are Captain James Smith's 4th New York Battery. They are pointing into a wood lot today, but those trees did not exist at the time of the battle. There were actually 700 yards of open fields from our position here to where the Confederates started on Seminary Ridge.

Two Confederate regiments—one from Texas and one from Arkansas—advance with about 900 men to this position, but they are beaten back. You have to understand that the Confederate advance that day against the

southern end of the Union battle line is an advance in echelon, like a wave attack. The first attack is against the far left of the Union battle line at Little Round Top and here at Devil's Den. Then the battle extends further to the north, to places like The Wheatfield, The Peach Orchard, and the Emmitsburg Road, where I showed you those two red barns along the sides of the road. Even though the Confederates are repulsed, another Confederate brigade always comes up on the left of the brigade just sent in. That's exactly what's taking place here. Henry Benning's 1,400 Georgia troops are now advancing, and they take a position to the right of the Texas and Arkansas troops, extending their line further to the right (to our left, about where the nose of the rocks is). That spot is called the nose of Devil's Den.

JOHN B. HOOD, CSA

Eventually two more Alabama regiments peel off from their attack on Little Round Top, coming down the slopes of Big Round Top into that low ground that you see just on the other side of these rocks—an area that we call The Slaughter Pen. Eventually the position is compromised. The Alabamans come in behind these guns; the Georgians come on the flank and in front of these guns; then Texas and Arkansas troops arrive off the flank of these guns. In a hand-to-hand fight, which compromises this position totally, three of these four guns are captured by the Confederates. They drive the Union soldiers from this position, back across the valley behind us, back to that hill—Little Round Top—that is 660 yards from our position.

When the Confederates are successful here, they set up sharpshooters—men with 35-pound heavy rifles, either Warner-Bench rifles from Philadelphia, or Whitworth rifles from Birmingham, England. These rifles are capable of firing up to 1,400 yards. At 35 pounds, they are heavy, and many a Confederate balances his gun on these rocks to fire at the Union forces on Little Round Top. They keep up their fire for the next two days with some very serious results. In fact, at the top of the hill, a Union general by the name of Stephen Weed is mortally wounded. The battery commander, Charles Hazlett (who also graduated with O'Rorke and Custer), is in charge of the guns on top of Little Round Top. He is almost instantly killed by a sharpshooter from these rocks. Even

General Warren, the following day (July 3rd) is shot in the throat (though he survives), taking his wound from a sharpshooter in Devil's Den.

To review, the Union position is in this direction, and the Confederates start attacking it in echelon. The next position to be attacked–and our next stop—is The Wheatfield, where more and more Confederates are attacking from south to north.

DEAD CONFEDERATE SHARPSHOOTER

THE WHEATFIELD TOWARDS LITTLE ROUND TOP

The events described in this tour occurred in the
Late Afternoon, July 2, 1863

The Wheatfield

ONE OF THE FIERCEST FIGHTS OF THE WAR LEAVES 6,000 DEAD AND WOUNDED AMONG THE WHEAT

We're in The Wheatfield now—right smack dab in the middle of The Wheatfield. Let me give you an idea of where we are and where we've been. Look down that road. It leads to Devil's Den. If you could look through these trees you'd be able to see the slopes of Little Round Top. Over your right shoulder, about 500 yards to your right, is The Peach Orchard, which we'll be getting into a little bit later.

This fight in The Wheatfield lasts about two-and-a-half hours, so there is some fighting in the Peach Orchard while this fight is going on, as well. This field changes hands unbelievably six different times that afternoon. Each side is trying to establish a defensive position along that stone wall that you see directly in your front, and also on the high ground just to its right. The Confederates call that area (to your right front) The Stony Hill because there were no trees on that high ground at that time. In fact, this would have been an open view for the cannons to fire at the Confederates coming in from that direction. The park has promised to get rid of those trees eventually. These are the guns of Winslow's Battery, which are pointing into open fields where the Confederates advance.

GEORGE B. WINSLOW, USA

As I said, this position changes hands six different times. Five different Confederate brigades enter this field and eventually implode the Union position that's in front of you. The men of Benning's Brigade are freed up from their attack against Devil's Den after they succeed in overrunning Devil's Den, and they arrive from that direction. George T. "Tige" Anderson's Georgians come in directly in front of us. Paul Semmes' brigade arrives from Anderson's left. To their left and gaining the high ground known as The Stony Hill, (or as we call it here at Gettysburg, The Loop), are Joseph Kershaw's South Carolinians.

Finally, the Union position in The Peach Orchard (on our right) breaks under the pressure of Confederate advances. That action frees up a Confederate brigade under the command of William Wofford to come into The Wheatfield almost unopposed. These guns (where we're standing right now) have been withdrawn, but the last attack by the Confederates comes from your right. When they arrive in this field, they find the Union position's rear and flank, and then these Union soldiers in front of us have to fight and withdraw under crossfire against five Confederate brigades.

PAUL J. SEMMES, CSA

To help facilitate the Union withdrawal from that little cul-de-sac directly in front of us, a brigade of U.S. Regulars—not U.S. Volunteers, but U.S. Regulars—under the command of Colonel Sidney Burbank, swing out and take a position along the ridgeline that runs through The Wheatfield (right where these monuments are). While these monuments are not dedicated to Sidney Burbank, they do mark his positions. These U.S. Regulars hold their fire; they have been brought into The Wheatfield to cover the retreat of the Union soldiers in their front. The Union soldiers fight to extricate themselves from the increasingly bad position, and they withdraw through the ranks of the U.S. Regulars, who are holding their fire. Finally the U.S. Regulars lower their weapons and fire volleys into the oncoming Confederates—five Confederate brigades. The final stand in The Wheatfield by any Union soldier is about where that last monument is in line—the position shared by the 10th and 11th U.S. Regulars. They stand there—the last to withdraw. They finally withdraw as a result of too many Confederates in their front, going hand-to-hand in that position until they are driven back across the valley (through those trees). They withdraw back across The Valley of Death, back to Little Round Top, with Confederates on their heels.

SIDNEY BURBANK, USA

Unfortunately for the Confederates, however, there is one last Union advance into this field from the slopes of Little Round Top. A group of Union soldiers called the Pennsylvania Reserves advance across the valley, hitting the Confederates in the valley and in those trees, driving them back across this field into the tree line on our right. At the end of the fight, the Confederates have possession of that tree line on your right, as well as the stone wall directly in front of us, while the Pennsylvania Reserves have the tree line and a stone wall to our left. It ended pretty much as a push that nobody really won. Nobody really lost The Wheatfield, either. There is a great deal of fire across this field for the next 24 hours. The wounded in this field suffer greatly as a result. Litter bearers are being shot down left, right, and sideways. As a result, some men actually bleed to death within 60 feet of their own lines. When it is all over, after some of the bloodiest fighting of the entire Civil War, there are approximately 6,000 dead and wounded in these 14 acres. They said you could walk from one end of the field to the other without ever touching the ground—just walking over the dead bodies.

THE PEACH ORCHARD TOWARDS BIG ROUND TOP

The events described in this tour occurred in the
Late Afternoon, July 2, 1863

The Peach Orchard
BARKSDALE'S CONFEDERATES SMASH INTO THE EXPOSED UNION LINE

Now we're in The Peach Orchard. This is the salient in Sickles' line. It bends back down along the Emmitsburg Road. Those are the two red barns I pointed to when we were up on Little Round Top. Sickles' right flank extends along the road, even past that last red barn. Then at The Peach Orchard it comes through the peach trees, all the way to the base of the Round Tops (Big and Little Round Top) in that direction. Very simply, a salient can always be attacked from two different directions, and that's one of the reasons why this position will fall. This also gives you a great view of the Confederate battle line, only 600 yards away. That tree line that you see in the distance is Seminary Ridge. It continues well to the south, and then it continues all the way to our north. The Confederate battle line on July 2nd attacks in echelon from that direction, south to north.

Now well to your left (past the Emmitsburg Road, in the distant tree line), Confederates advance from those positions to go up and over Big Round Top to attack Little Round Top. A bit further up the line to our right, Confederates advance from those positions when they overrun Devil's Den. More Confederates are attacking a bit farther up the line to our right—Confederates who are entering The Wheatfield and attacking the Union position (at least in the initial stages in The Wheatfield).

JOSEPH B. KERSHAW, CSA

Then we have another Confederate brigade, which really is the "fly in the ointment" here. That is Joseph Kershaw's South Carolina brigade, which starts approximately where that park tower now stands (called the Confederate Tower, the Longstreet Tower, or the Eisenhower Tower because on the other side of that tower is where the Eisenhower farm is). Kershaw's Brigade advances across these open fields, from the tower across these fields, past the southern end of The Peach Orchard on our left. That maneuver forces the Union soldiers in this area to train their attention upon Kershaw's Brigade. Many a Union outfit advances from this road intersection where we're located now, through the peach trees to the south end of The Peach Orchard, to confront Kershaw's Brigade. However, Kershaw's Brigade continues on. It takes the fire of the Union soldiers and continues on to engage in The Wheatfield, about 500 yards in that direction through these peach trees.

However, while this is going on, the in-echelon attack by the Confederates continues, and William Barksdale's brigade then advances. Barksdale advances the 600 yards at double-quick, taking only minutes to get from that tree line to where we stand right now. In fact, he has 1,800 men moving at a fast pace on a 300 yard front, and it is his luck to catch the Union position at its weakest point, from the intersection of this road (the Millerstown/Wheatfield Road and the Emmitsburg Road) to those buildings on your right (the Scherfy farm complex). Barksdale breaks the Union position there. All the

WILLIAM BARKSDALE, CSA

Union soldiers at the southern end of The Peach Orchard (on our left) are forced to abandon their positions and hastily make a new line where those monuments are back there. In fact, most of the fighting in The Peach Orchard actually takes place on that second defensive position. These positions are very poorly placed—they have no fence lines, no constructions of any sort. As Barksdale's Brigade comes swinging in with momentum (and very few casualties along the way), it comes up and over the ridgeline, hitting the Union position—that second position of the Union soldiers from The Peach Orchard—and breaking that position in detail (bit by bit), to send the Union soldiers back to that tree line in the distance.

The gap here is expanded laterally at this point. William Wofford's brigade is right behind William Barksdale's brigade, and Wofford is sent right through the peach trees here to continue on, unopposed, into The Wheatfield. If you remember, the Confederates came through those woods unopposed into the rear of the Union position in

The Wheatfield, completely compromising that position. Then Barksdale's Brigade expands the gap to the left, as well, and heads north with its left flank resting on the Emmitsburg Road, while more Confederates advance across these open fields. They arrive in echelon—Wilcox's Brigade, Lang's Brigade of Floridians, Wright's Brigade, Posey's Brigade—advancing from left to right, always with Barksdale's Brigade pushing up the road, as well. All the Union soldiers along the Emmitsburg Road are compromised, literally, by being attacked from two different directions, always with a portion of Barksdale's Brigade coming up the road and the ever-increasing Confederate brigades advancing the 600 yards from Seminary Ridge. That's how close Sickles has advanced his men to the enemy position. As they hit from the west, Barksdale hits from the south. Every outfit on this road breaks down from left to right, stretching all the way down into the 2nd Corps positions of Winfield Scott Hancock.

EMMITSBURG ROAD—LOOKING NORTH

The events described in this tour occurred in the
Late Afternoon, July 2, 1863

Emmitsburg Road

CONFEDERATES MOMENTARILY BREACH UNION LINE ON CEMETERY RIDGE

Coming down the Emmitsburg Road is a portion of Barksdale's Brigade, which has broken the Union position at The Peach Orchard. Not only do the Confederates push through the gap that they create, but they also try to expand the gap laterally, with the help of an Alabama brigade on their left flank under the command of Brigadier General Cadmus Wilcox. Cadmus Wilcox's brigade advances from the west and goes right through that farmhouse (the Klingle farm). Their advance comes through there, with Barksdale's Brigade to their right (closer to the Round Tops). This is the gap the Confederates create—almost a quarter of a mile here—as they drive the Union soldiers back through the woods to our front. Those woods (the Trostle Wood Lot) were here at the time of the battle, but they were a lot thinner than they are today. That's pretty much where the Confederate advance stalls, to some extent.

CADMUS M. WILCOX, CSA

At one point during the battle, Winfield Scott Hancock, the Union commander of the 2nd Corps, is ordered by George Gordon Meade to try to shore up the Union left flank the best he possibly can. Hancock fans out his artillery with some infantry support in an attempt to do just that. The most famous combination of artillery and infantry is probably Thomas' Battery, with the 1st Minnesota in support, which is positioned approximately where the Pennsylvania Memorial is today. To our right, Barksdale's Brigade pushes in toward those woods. To their left is Cadmus Wilcox's brigade heading for Thomas' Battery, approximately where the Pennsylvania Memorial now stands.

EVAN THOMAS, USA

However, both brigades run into a problem. Not only does Winfield Scott Hancock send out some infantry and artillery to guard his left flank; he also sends a brigade under the command of Colonel George Willard. Willard's Brigade comes bounding out of those woods, hitting Barksdale's Brigade. In fact, Barksdale's Brigade—an overachiever to this point—is finally driven back. The last time anyone sees Barksdale on his horse is on the high ground (just to the right of the cattle) where he is trying to rally the 13th, the 17th, and the 18th Mississippi regiments. Unfortunately, Barksdale is shot off his horse by either the 125th or the 126th New York from Willard's Brigade. With their commander down, Barksdale's men withdraw.

GEORGE L. WILLARD, USA

On their left, however, Wilcox's Brigade continues on, heading toward Thomas' Battery (close to where the Pennsylvania Memorial stands today). At this point, Winfield Scott Hancock, seeing exactly what is taking place, orders the 264 men of the 1st Minnesota to affix bayonets and charge approximately 1,400 Alabamans heading toward Thomas' Brigade. They meet at the headwaters of Plum Run Valley (at the edge of these trees), and in a fight that lasts probably 15 minutes; the Minnesotans lose 234 men out of 264 that charged. In fact, the 84% loss of the 1st Minnesota is the highest percentage loss of any Union regiment—not only at Gettysburg, but also in the entire war. However, it is not only the charge of the 1st Minnesota that drives Wilcox's Brigade back. When Willard's Brigade is successful against Barksdale, it turns on the flank and threatens the rear of Wilcox's Brigade. Thus Wilcox's Brigade is not only attacked from the front, but also from the flank and rear by Willard's Brigade. Finally Wilcox withdraws.

There are other Confederate brigades attacking Wilcox's left, but they don't fare much better. David Lang's Floridians are about halfway across this field (approximately where that fallen tree is, in the middle of the field) before they are driven back. However, there is one over-achieving Confederate brigade of Georgians under the command of a brigadier general by the name of Ambrose R. Wright, that actually pierces the Union battle line (where that obelisk can be seen in the distance—the Army of the Potomac Monument). Wright claimed that he and his brigade got to within sight of George Gordon Meade's headquarters, but he probably penetrated the line to about 100 yards inside the Union artillery line along Cemetery Ridge. Then looking to his right and seeing Wilcox's and Lang's brigades withdraw, and seeing no support on his left flank, Wright is forced to withdraw as he sees more and more Union reinforcements arriving at his front. This is the last attack against the Union left flank—the farthest the Confederates actually get to Cemetery Ridge. With no support, however, they are forced to withdraw.

You're in a very unusual position, very close to the Emmitsburg Road (we're just on the east side of it). There are two five-foot fences here—one on either side of the road—that the Confederates have to negotiate, not only on July 2nd, but also on July 3rd. We're in front of something called the Rogers Farm, which no longer exists, but a white picket fence indicates the boundary of the Rogers Farm front yard. It is here, on July 3rd, that James Kemper's brigade, of George Pickett's division, crosses the road and starts to oblique hard to the left, paralleling the road and heading for The Angle. You can see the clump of trees, and just to the left of that is The Angle, which is significant, as well. George Pickett and four of his staff members, all on horseback, get to approximately the position where the camera is standing right now. This is his view of Pickett's Charge on that fateful day of July 3rd, 1863, when Robert E. Lee issues orders for almost 13,000 Confederates to advance toward the Union center.

UNION BREASTWORKS ON CULP'S HILL

The events described in this tour occurred in the
Evening, July 2, 1863

Culp's Hill

DESPERATE EVENING ATTACK AGAINST UNION RIGHT FLANK FOILED BY BREASTWORKS

You are now on the Union right flank. This is Culp's Hill—the point of the hook. Culp's Hill did not look this way at the time of the battle. Then the hill was pasture area for sheep and goats that ate all the sapling growth, the secondary growth. At that time, the only growth on this hill was the large trees. You actually had a pretty good line of sight then from the bottom of the hill right up to the top of the hill, which, as you can see, no longer exists.

HENRY W. SLOCUM, USA

In the afternoon of July 2nd, there will be approximately 5,000 Confederates attacking this hill. Earlier in the day, however, the Union commander at Gettysburg, George Gordon Meade, is very worried that Robert E. Lee is going to attack him on this hill. Meade therefore places 10,000 Union soldiers on top of this hill—the entire Union 12th Corps under the command of a major general by the name of Henry Slocum. Of course, you'd say to yourself, if 5,000 Confederates attack uphill toward 10,000 Union soldiers, then the Confederates simply won't have a very good chance of success on this hill—and you'd be right.

However, something very unusual happens here that gives the Confederates a much better opportunity. The uncoordinated Confederate attack against both ends of the Union battle line that day (July 2nd), actually bene-fits the Confederates at this end. It's now approximately five o'clock in the afternoon. The attack against the other end of the Union battle line—places like Little Round Top and Devil's Den (about two-and-a-half miles from here)—has been going on for approximately one hour. Those attacks by the Confederates began at 4:00 PM.

By five o'clock in the afternoon, things are not looking very good on the slopes of Little Round Top and Devil's Den for the Union army. George Gordon Meade, the Union commander, is desperately seeking Union reinforcements. He needs men to send down to the other end. At approximately five o'clock in the afternoon, orders are given that Henry Slocum should start abandoning this hill and sending his brigades down to support the Union left flank. All but one are withdrawn from this hill, leaving 1,500 Union soldiers under the command of a brigadier general from the state of New York by the name of George Greene on top of this hill throughout the day. It's fortunate that his position is the top of the hill. During the day, George Greene has been constructing

GEORGE S. GREENE, USA

fortifications—log walls. He calls his walls a traversing breastwork—that is, a series of log walls, standing anywhere from three-and-a-half to five feet in height and stretching almost 550 yards in length.

The men who are building these fortifications—New Yorkers all—are none too happy about the task. They are moaning and groaning and complaining throughout the day. They see no need for it, since they are building these fortifications when there are 10,000 Union soldiers on top of the hill. These same 1,500 Union soldiers who complain so bitterly are darn happy that they do build these fortifications because, when 8,500 Union soldiers are withdrawn, the remaining troops now have a way of defending the top of this hill. The fortifications in front of you will make the difference between winning and losing for the Union army on that evening of July 2nd, 1863. George Greene's fortifications—his traverse—begin about where the park road is. Look to your left, past that stump, through that stone, to the corner of the woods, and then at right-angles up the hill until, if you look forward, you'll see a mound of ground right at the tree line. The ground looks like a gopher mound with leaves piled on top of it. That's what the remnants of his fortifications look like today. You have to imagine the sight: that mound of ground, log on top of log on top of log standing anywhere from three-and-a-half feet to five feet in height, a dirt ditch dug on this side of it for the Union soldier to stand in (the dirt thrown up on those logs), and 1,500 Union soldiers fighting in single-file, starting here and stretching up the hill, 550 yards up and over the other side of the hill. Those New Yorkers are resting their rifles on those fortifications and firing down over them into the tree line in front of us at 5,000 Confederates coming up the hill at them.

The Confederates attack this hill for almost three hours with no success whatsoever. They can't get within 60 yards of any portion of George Greene's defenses—that's how well they are built, and that's how well his men fight for them. The Confederates lose nearly 800 men in killed and wounded trying to push George Greene and his New York brigade off the top of this hill. George Greene loses exactly 303 of his Union soldiers in the defense of the Union right flank.

Now Robert E. Lee himself said, had he had victory at *either* end of the Union battle line on that July 2nd— either at Little Round Top or here at Culp's Hill—it may well have resulted in Southern independence within six weeks. That makes these hill fights at Gettysburg very, very important and some of the most studied military actions in the world.

CEMETERY HILL FROM STEVEN'S KNOLL

The events described in this tour occurred in the
Late Evening, July 2, 1863

Cemetery Hill ∽

LOUISIANA TIGERS END SECOND DAY'S FIGHTING WITH RARE NIGHT ATTACK AGAINST UNION CANNONS

We're on Cemetery Hill, the rallying point of the Union soldier on the evening of July 1st. It is also the site of a Confederate attack on the evening of July 2nd. To your right is Culp's Hill. That attack has been going on for a number of hours before this attack begins. In fact, the Confederates attack this position literally in total darkness, which is a rarity in the American Civil War. You generally do not attack or defend at night. The Confederates advance against this hill, which has been made a very strong Union position by the addition of over 40 Union cannons. Now the Confederates advance across these fields to the east of us (in your front and to your left), coming out of the town, itself, from the northeast. The Confederates pounce on this position, breaking the

R. BRUCE RICKETTS, USA

Union battle line at the base of the hill, and they ascend the slopes into these guns. The Confederates reach six guns—four of Michael Wiedrich's guns and the left section of Bruce Ricketts' guns—and there is hand-to-hand fighting at the guns. The cannoneers, however, do not give up these guns willingly, in any way, shape or form.

Finally, Winfield Scott Hancock, near the Union center, sends 2nd Corps reinforcements—not only to Culp's Hill to reinforce George Greene, but also to this hill. He sends Colonel Samuel Carroll's brigade. They call him "Red" Carroll (he had red hair), and Carroll's brigade forms in the cemetery (the Evergreen Cemetery, the old town cemetery across the Baltimore Pike), charging across the road in battle line (just

SAMUEL "RED" CARROLL, USA

south of the gatehouse). They hit the Confederates at these guns and, at the point of a bayonet, drive them out of these guns and back down the hill. It's an interesting battle in that it is initiated by the Confederates in total darkness. Both sides dislike fighting at night for various reasons: the darkness of the night, itself; the smoke that a battle generates, especially on a calm evening (and it was a calm evening that night, though for another reason). Most soldiers, both North and South, suffered night blindness from the deficiency of two particular vitamins in their diet—A and D—which causes night blindness. You and I can see in the dark a great deal farther and a great deal better than the common soldier in 1863. As a result, it is a very scary affair to attack or defend in a night battle. This is one of the rare occurrences when the Confederates initiate an attack in total darkness.

When they tabulate the casualties that day, there are almost 21,000 combined—both North and South on July 2nd. It turns out to be one of the bloodiest days of the entire Civil War. The Confederates had tried both ends of the Union battle line on July 2nd—coming close at both ends because major mistakes were made by Union leaders at both ends. Other Union commanders, often of lesser rank, had stepped forward, however, and made up for the mistakes of others. At the close of battle, the Union battle line is still very much in the shape of the "fishhook", and it is now very secure at both ends. Robert E. Lee has lost approximately 20,000 men up to that point in the fighting on July 1st and 2nd. He no longer has the option of just walking away from this battlefield, claiming it a draw or any form of victory. If he is to attack again, he's going to have to attack somewhere else, and he will choose the Union center—what he believes to be a weaker point in the Union battle line, which will culminate in something that we call Pickett's Charge on July 3rd.

LOOKING NORTH-EAST OVER GROUND OCCUPIED BY LOUISIANA TIGERS

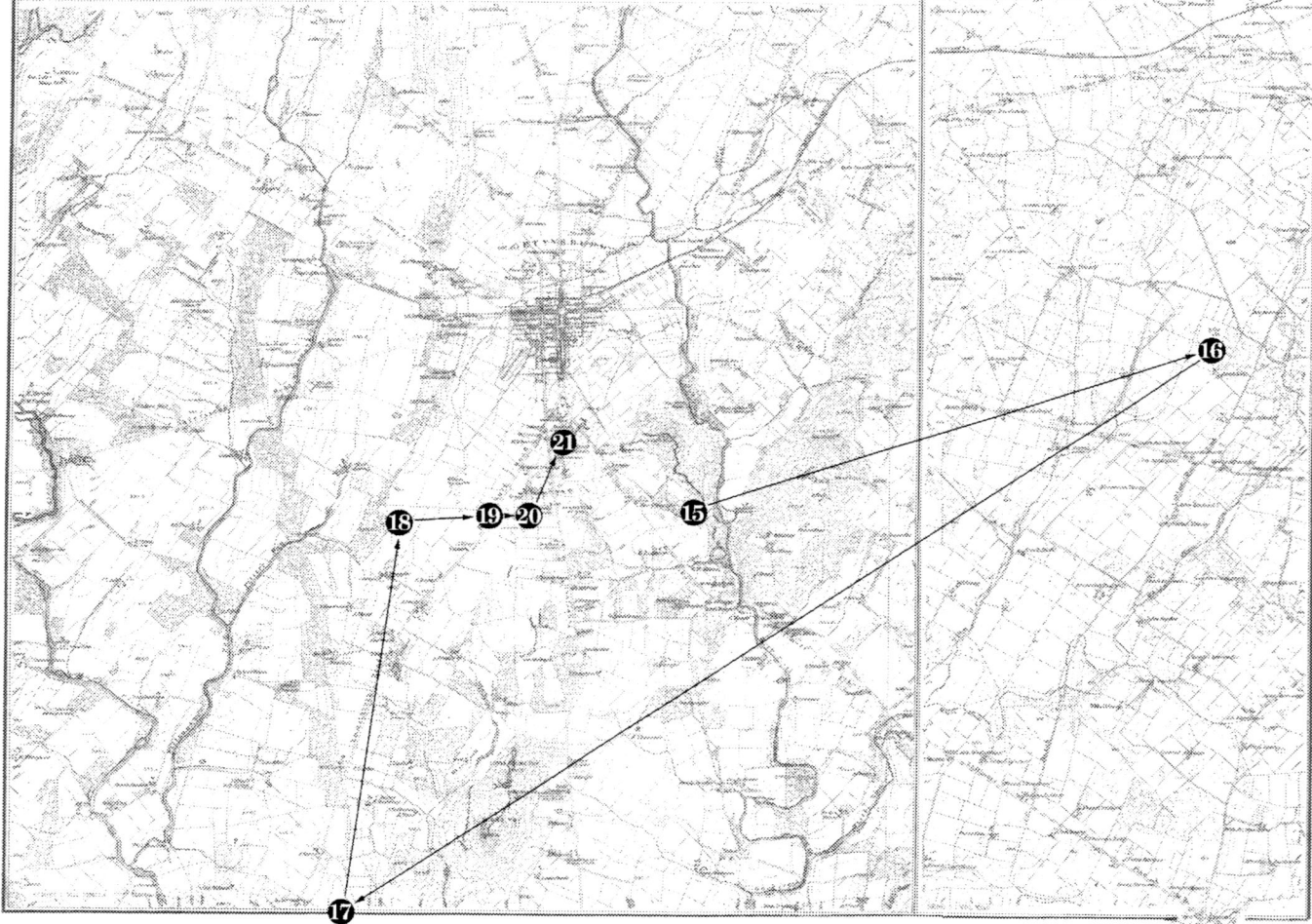

Audio **3** Tour

SPANGLER'S SPRING

The events described in this tour occurred in the
Early Morning, July 3, 1863

Spangler's Spring

EARLY MORNING UNION ATTACK IS LONGEST SUSTAINED ACTION AT GETTYSBURG

Now we are at the base of Culp's Hill, the scene of the action on July 3rd—the third day of the Battle of Gettysburg. We're at a place called Spangler's Spring. It is a water source for both Union and Confederate soldiers during the battle on July 2nd and 3rd. When the Confederates press the Union left flank on the afternoon and early evening of July 2nd—the Union left flank at Devil's Den and Little Round Top—George Gordon Meade pulls from his right to reinforce his left. As we were discussing, only one brigade is left on top of this hill—George Greene's brigade. The 8,500 Union soldiers that are in and around this hill, especially the bottom part of the hill, are withdrawn and sent to other portions of the battlefield, leaving the bottom part of the hill unoccupied.

When the Confederates advance that evening against George Greene's brigade on the top of the hill, many Confederates just slide down the hill and occupy the lower portion of the hill, as well, and they entrench there that night. Their entrenchments can still be seen—these rocks here, that stone wall to our left, and more in this tree line on some high ground. They also entrench along a stone wall on the other side of that meadow that you see in the distance (the Spangler Meadow). In fact, by the time those 8,500 Union soldiers start to return to this area, they bump into the Confederates at these points and take a parallel position behind us, down toward the Baltimore Pike (about 300 yards in that direction), to the high ground that you see to our left (McCalister's Woods). Thus the Union position is actually parallel to the Confederate position; they could go no farther.

However, it is determined by the Union hierarchy that the Confederates are way too close to the Union flank—within yards of George Greene's position on top of the hill. It is decided that when these Union soldiers return, they will "press the envelope" the following morning with an artillery barrage to start as early as 4:00 AM, at a place called Power's Hill (high ground on the other side of the Baltimore Pike). That attack will be the longest sustained action at Gettysburg. Union soldiers now start attacking the base of this hill, trying to regain what they gave away the night before.

Probably the most famous charge is made across Spangler's Meadow by two Union regiments—the 2nd Massachusetts and the 27th Indiana—which attack in two different directions. The 2nd Massachusetts charges toward us under the command of Lieutenant Colonel Charles R. Mudge, who calls his orders "murder." That description will prove somewhat prophetic because Mudge is mortally wounded in these rocks right here in front of us. The 27th Indiana charges across that field. Where you see that little plug in the ground (in the middle of the field) is about as close to the base of Culp's Hill as they get before they are shot down. They withdraw. There are not too many offensive actions at Gettysburg by the Union army. This is one of them, and it is ill-conceived right from the start, costing both regiments almost 50% of their personnel.

CHARLES R. MUDGE, USA

This happens about six o'clock in the morning. Pardee Field happens about nine o'clock in the morning. On the other side of the Confederate entrenchments (directly in front of us) is another field—Ario Pardee Field. It is named after the lieutenant colonel of the 147th Pennsylvania, Ario Pardee, who, in the middle of the night, is ordered to move forward to feel out the Confederate force in his front. He is successful in gaining a wall and holding on to that wall for much of the morning. In fact, as the Confederates continue their attack against George Greene and all the reinforcements that have come to Greene during that night, Pardee always finds himself on the flank of the Confederates who are attacking the top of the hill. Then he places himself in a very advantageous position, and the Confederates finally—in their third attempt—turn their attention against him and push him back across the field. He very brazenly calls the field "Ario Pardee Field" because

ARIO PARDEE, USA

he believes that he was there the longest (and he certainly was) and that he did very good work for the Union army, firing into the flank of the Confederates attacking the top, or upper portion of the hill.

The entire hill is attacked by the Confederates in various ways. Not only are the Union soldiers trying to drive the Confederates from the base of the hill, but Confederates are also trying to renew the attack toward the top of the hill. Greene has been relieved by the addition of other Union brigades at this point. The 147th Pennsylvania (and Ario Pardee,) find themselves on the flank of those Confederate attacks. With the help of Pardee, and because of the way that George Greene has constructed his fortifications that are still in Union hands, the Confederates have no opportunity to push the Union soldiers off. When you really think about it, the Confederates could not push off 1,500 Union soldiers the night of July 2nd. There are over 10,000 Union infantry in this area on July 3rd, and if there was any hope to have success on the Union right flank, it would have been the night of July 2nd against George Greene's command.

By the morning of July 3rd, there is no longer an opportunity for the Confederates to be successful here. They try until eleven o'clock in the morning, but when they realize it is no longer achievable, they withdraw across Rock Creek (in that direction) back to their starting points. What's interesting about this affair is that when the morning begins, Robert E. Lee is hoping that during the time of Pickett's Charge, the entire Union battle line will be ablaze. He hopes that there will be fighting everywhere, that Union reinforcements can not be pulled from this area to reinforce the Union center, that Union reinforcements facing the Confederates—at Devil's Den, for instance, and Confederates at one point have half of The Wheatfield—will also be attacked, and that the entire Union battle line will be ablaze. Then Robert E. Lee can amass 13,000 men and push them forward across almost a mile of open ground, with no Union reinforcements coming from the flanks to reinforce the Union center.

Unfortunately, because of the timetables, with Union soldiers at both ends—here at Culp's Hill pushing the envelope at four o'clock in the morning—by eleven o'clock in the morning, the Confederates have already abandoned the attempt and withdrawn. There are now 10,000 Union soldiers available to reinforce the Union center if necessary. Three o'clock in the afternoon, you have Union cavalry down at the other end harassing the Confederate right flank. The Confederates then, instead of renewing their attack against places like Little Round Top and The Wheatfield, or advancing their artillery even closer to the Union position, now have to worry about a cavalry threat on their own right flank and rear. As a result, at one o'clock in the afternoon when the Confederates began their artillery barrage against the Union center, and by three o'clock in the afternoon when they begin the infantry assault, the only action that is actually taking place is the advance by 13,000 Confederates across a mile of open ground. That means that all the attention of the Union soldiers can be focused on the one Confederate assault that defines the third day at Gettysburg—Pickett's Charge.

SPANGLER'S MEADOW FROM POSITION OF 2ND MASSACHUSETTS

THE RUMMEL FARM

The events described in this tour occurred in the
Afternoon, July 3, 1863

East Cavalry Field

JEB STUART'S CONFEDERATE CAVALRY MEETS GENERAL GEORGE ARMSTRONG CUSTER

Now we are on the East Cavalry Battlefield. It's somewhat separate from the regular battle-field. We're four-and-a-half miles away from the battlefield of Gettysburg. General J. E. B. (Jeb) Stuart, commander of Robert E. Lee's cavalry, has been out of contact with Lee's army for almost three days. As a result, when he arrives at Gettysburg, he finds that Lee has no plans for him for any meaningful action, not even in the coordinating action to George Pickett's advance across a mile of open ground against the Union center.

J.E.B. "JEB" STUART, CSA

The action here takes place about the same time as Pickett's Charge but it has nothing to do with Pickett's Charge. The only order that Lee gives Stuart is to guard the Confederate left flank—Richard Ewell's forces. However, Jeb Stuart, to "press the envelope," has been pushing farther and farther away from the Confederate left flank, looking to run into some-thing. He knows the Union cavalry screen is out here somewhere. In my opinion, he keeps looking until he finds it; and he finds it on this position.

To give you an idea just how far away from the battlefield we actually are, and how far away the cavalry screens of both armies engage, look in that direction where you can see Big Round Top, well in the distance. The "fish-hook" line is in that direction—the end of the line. Then it goes to the right (which you can't see because of the intervening high ground), ending somewhere in the distance past that red barn. We are four-and-a-half miles away from the battlefield, itself. This is where the two cavalry screens bump into each other—where George Armstrong Custer meets Jeb Stuart. Stuart arrives here with his horse artillery and four brigades of cavalry.

From left to right are: up in Cress Ridge, General Fitzhugh Lee's cavalry; to his right, General Wade Hampton's cavalry; to his right, Colonel John Chambliss' brigade; and to his right, General A. G. Jenkins' brigade. General Jenkins is wounded as soon as he arrives at Gettysburg, and as a result, his brigade is under the command of a lieutenant colonel by the name of Vincent Witcher. The line therefore includes Fitz Lee, Hampton, Chambliss, and Witcher's Brigades pushed out in front of those woods (the Cress Woods on Cress Ridge) with Stuart's horse artillery.

GEORGE A. CUSTER, USA

The reason the Union cavalry is out this far is that it is guarding one of only two roads that lead into the rear of the Union position—the Union "fishhook" line. One of those roads is the Low Dutch Road which, if you follow it, continues all the way to the Baltimore Pike, which runs right in behind the Union battle line. The Union position is an "L" configuration. That water tower is very close to the Hanover Road, which is guarded by Custer's command. In this "L" configuration, coming up the Low Dutch Road (from right to left) and ending in these woods, is John McIntosh's brigade (900 more Union cavalry).

The lines are drawn here at this point. The battle begins in a very meek way with two dismounted skirmishing actions. First, Jeb Stuart sends a portion of Witcher's Brigade forward, to take position in and around the buildings of the Rummel Farm (just on the other side of the second tree line directly in front of us). Union soldiers from John McIntosh's command advance dismounted across these open fields, taking a position in that tree line overlooking the Rummel Farmhouse and the Confederate skirmish line.

These men fight each other on foot for about an hour. The Union skirmishers begin to run out of ammunition, and they start withdrawing back across these open fields. Jeb Stuart perceives the move as a sign of weakness, and he orders two Confederate regiments from John Chambliss' command (the 9th and 13th Virginia Cavalry) to charge the retreating Union soldiers across this field and to get behind the rest of the Union skirmish line still fighting along that little ridge line.

FITZHUGH LEE, CSA

While this was going on, however, the Union commanders are well aware that their skirmish line is breaking down, so George Armstrong Custer sends forward the 5th Michigan Cavalry, dismounted. They elongate the line (to the left of the park road where those evergreen trees are along the top of that ridge). However, as they take position, the 9th and 13th Virginia swing behind and hit the 5th Michigan. It is quite a fight. Where the park road can be seen today, the 5th Michigan's right flank is refused as a result of this cavalry charge across that open field. There are about 50 casualties in the 5th Michigan.

However, the 5th Michigan does some damage to the 9th and 13th Virginia, as well. The 5th Michigan is one of two regiments that Custer has supplied with Spencer repeating rifles, known as the Yankee guns that can be loaded on Sunday and fired all week (seven shots in the magazine and one in the chamber before you have to reload). This repeating rifle is the pre-cursor of the Winchester.

This is quite a heated battle between the 5th Michigan of Custer's command, fighting dismounted, and the mounted men of the 9th and 13th Virginia, just in and around the park road and slightly to the left of it. Custer realizes that his 5th Michigan is in peril at this point. Custer rides to the 7th Michigan Cavalry at the Spangler Farm (about where that distant water tower can be seen), then pulls up in front of it, draws his Toledo Blade, and yells "Charge!" His men charge in battle line across these open fields. The 9th and 13th Virginia Cavalry see 500 men in battle line charging, and they have no stomach for the fight, so they withdraw.

While all this is going on, another Confederate regiment enters the fight. The 1st Virginia Cavalry has come from Fitz Lee's position (the far right portion of Cress Ridge), and most of the command dismounts along a very substantial stone wall (the first line of scrub trees that you see directly in front of us). The dismounted soldiers of the 9th and 13th Virginia are still lingering in the area behind them. Now Custer and the 7th Michigan are charging to the point where we're standing right now. They look forward and see that substantial stone wall with Confederate cavalry behind it, but they continue to charge. They engage the Confederate cavalry at that wall for a number of minutes, while being shot at by the 9th and 13th Virginia, as well as the dismounted men of the 1st Virginia. Custer's men cannot get across the wall.

Stuart now sees an opportunity to take advantage of a Union regiment in a precarious situation. He sends reinforcements into the fight—the 1st North Carolina and the Jeff Davis Legion. They charge from the Cress Woods (behind the 1st Virginia), parallel to the 1st Virginia, trying to swing up and around the left flank of Custer, who is still fighting in the field in front of us. Custer immediately orders his men back, with the order, "Men, we must get behind our guns." He heads for the guns—four cannons loaded with canister, which are part of McIntosh's command. The Confederates are in close pursuit. As Custer's men get near the guns, however, they veer hard to the right. Then the guns open fire on the oncoming Confederates, emptying many a Confederate saddle. These Confederates now withdraw back where they started, not only past the stone wall, but all the way back to Cress Ridge. Finally there is a lull in the battle.

George Armstrong Custer then rides back in front of the 1st Michigan Cavalry (500-600 men) and charges in this direction yet again. Seeing this, Stuart orders 1,500 Confederates to draw up along Cress Ridge, draw their sabers in battle line, and charge in this direction. The two cavalry forces meet on this exact spot where a melee takes place for approximately ten minutes. Their line stretches to our left and right. The left flank of the Confederate advance from Cress Ridge is right about where that monument (the Gregg Cavalry Shaft) has a fence around it. For ten minutes, Custer's men are totally engulfed—only 500-600 men are battling 1,500 Confederates.

Then help arrives from two areas: from Custer's command closer to the Hanover Road (the 5th Michigan, now mounted and with their Spencer repeating rifles); and from the Lott Woods, two charges (the 1st New Jersey and the 3rd Pennsylvania Cavalry). The final charge pretty much determines the outcome when a small portion of the 3rd Pennsylvania Cavalry, under the command of Captain William Miller (the only man on this field that day to win the Congressional Medal of Honor), charges both the flank and the rear of the Confederate line. The Confederates, perceiving that their way of retreat may be blocked by more and more Union soldiers charging from the Lott Woods, now start to separate.

WILLIAM MILLER, USA

This fight lasts for only ten minutes, but it's one of the great melees—saber against saber, pistol against pistol, and carbine against carbine—causing about 600 casualties on this field. Custer is de-horsed on the spot where we're standing. Just to our left is where Wade Hampton takes a revolver ball in his hip and is slashed over his eyes by a saber. Near the Gregg Cavalry Shaft, Fitzhugh Lee finds himself in a death-dealing duel with a soldier from the 1st New Jersey. While nothing happens to Fitz Lee, he comes very, very close to capture at that point.

WADE HAMPTON, CSA

These two sides then just simply part, both claiming victory here at East Cavalry Battlefield. Stuart found his battle, but nothing really was accomplished. You have two glory hunters—Stuart and Custer—meeting on this field in one of the great cavalry engagements of the war. When 1,500 Confederate cavalry charged 500-600 Union cavalry, there must have been thunder here, with the sabers flashing in the sunlight. This is the Michigan monument depicting a typical Michigan cavalry trooper. Custer had only taken command of the Michigan brigade a few days earlier, being promoted, along with Elon Farnsworth and Wesley Merritt on the 28th of June. By July 3rd, he has not been a general very long.

There's a great story about Custer. When he was told that he was made brigadier general, he went out and had a suit made for himself—a dark blue or black velveteen uniform with gold braid from his collar to his cuffs. He wore that uniform with a large white plantation hat and a big red bandana around his throat. He also rode a thoroughbred black horse. The first time these dirty old soldiers from the Michigan brigade (and they had been in it from the very start, serving in many, many a battle) laid eyes on their new brigadier general, one of the men called him "a circus rider gone mad." But after Custer personally led the two charges at Gettysburg, the next review of the 1st, 5th, 6th, and 7th Michigan Cavalry before their general, found almost every rider sporting a red bandana around his throat as a token of respect to the new general. Custer had proven himself one of the finest cavalry commanders of the war—certainly one of the bravest.

BIG ROUND TOP FROM THE SOUTH WEST

The events described in this tour occurred in the
Afternoon, July 3, 1863

South Cavalry Field

ILL-FATED UNION CAVALRY CHARGE AGAINST CONFEDERATE RIGHT FLANK

Now we're at the south end of the battlefield, just off the right flank of the Confederate battle line (in front of us). The battle line continues in that direction (north), and it is opposite the Union battle line that is anchored on those hills—Big and Little Round Top. The Confederates, after being pushed off both Little Round Top and Big Round Top, assume the position halfway up the southern and southwestern slopes of Big Round Top (facing us right now). They fortify their position with a stone wall, occupying all the natural fortifications that they can possibly use on the hill. They set up a skirmish line with a reasonably heavy Confederate concentration on and around the base of Big Round Top. It then goes to our left, linking up with the rest of the Confederate battle line. It is this area that 3,200 Union cavalry try to exploit on the afternoon of July 3rd.

JUDSON KILPATRICK, USA

As early as one o'clock in the afternoon, 1,900 men with four cannons are ordered up this valley on our right to get as close to the Confederate-occupied portions of Big Round Top as possible. They are under the command of a brigadier general by the name of Elon Farnsworth, who is under the orders of Brigadier General Judson Kilpatrick. These men push the Confederate skirmishers back through the valley on our right to a hill called Bushman Hill. The hill is just this side of Big Round Top and kind of blends in. This spot is where the four guns of Elder's U.S. Battery are placed in support of a charge that will be made against the fortified Confederate positions on Big Round Top later in the day.

WESLEY MERRITT, USA

Two hours later, things start to heat up when, coming down the Emmitsburg Road on our left, is another Union brigade under the command of Brigadier General Wesley Merritt. Merritt's men stop approximately where we are right now and fan out on foot into the open fields to take on the skirmish line, trying to swing in to the rear of the Confederate position. Both charges fail. Elon Farnsworth has not wanted to make the charge, but Judson Kilpatrick orders him to make a mounted charge against those very heavily fortified positions of the Confederates halfway up Big Round Top. At that time, Big Round Top was not as wooded as it is today; much of the base of the hill was open, but the ground was too rocky and too wooded for a mounted charge. In addition, the Confederates have built some rather strong fortifications halfway up the hill. Elon Farnsworth protests, but then Kilpatrick suggests that he, himself, will lead the charge, and Farnsworth acquiesces, feeling that if anybody can succeed, it will be Farnsworth.

Farnsworth leads the charge against those Confederate positions, actually breaking through the skirmish line and advancing up the slopes of Big Round Top, only to be shot back. It is a costly measure for Elon Farnsworth, who is riddled with four or five bullets. His body is found the following day, and he becomes one of nine generals killed at the Battle of Gettysburg.

Merritt fares no better on our left. General Merritt's men, on some of the best ground to make a mounted cavalry charge (remember, he advanced his men on foot), cannot get around the Confederate skirmish line to threaten the Confederate rear. In the end, both charges fail. In all, there are 3,200 Union cavalrymen plus ten cannons (four with Elder, and six more in Capt. William Graham's Battery, where we're standing) firing in support of both actions—all of them harassing the Confederate right flank. These are meaningful actions down here, and we view them separately: Merritt's action called the South Cavalry Battlefield; the other called Farnsworth's Charge. While both

ELON J. FARNSWORTH, USA

actions fail, they do occupy the Confederates' attention during those very crucial hours between one o'clock and five o'clock in the afternoon on July 3rd, when another action at the Union center takes place—Pickett's Charge.

When we view Civil War battles today with the benefit of 20/20 hindsight, and we analyze the Battle of Gettysburg, it is easy to say that Farnsworth and Merritt's charges were needless actions in light of the Confederate defeat at the hands of General Winfield Scott Hancock and the 2nd Corps the same day against the Union center. However, when this cavalry charge is made, the issue is still in doubt, and Lee does not retreat from Meade's front until the following day. Both sides are looking for an advantage anywhere they can find it. At the time, Judson Kilpatrick is looking to create such an advantage, but Farnsworth's Charge proves too high a price for what is gained. It could have been a very meaningful action against the Confederate right flank, however, had it succeeded.

LOOKING NORTH TOWARDS THE SPANGLER FARM

The events described in this tour occurred in the
Afternoon, July 3, 1863

Point of Woods

CONFEDERATES ARRAY FOR ATTACK AS CANNONADE PRECEDES EPIC CHARGE

We are now at a place called the Point of Woods—the location where Robert E. Lee viewed Pickett's Charge, the grand assault against the Union center on July 3rd. Today it's called Pickett's Charge (named after Major General George Pickett), but it should really not be. First, Pickett had very little to do with the decision but was only following orders to move forward. After the war, Virginians had a nasty habit, when they were writing the history of the war, of naming events after Virginians; and Pickett was the only major general from Virginia who was in that charge.

This key event should really be called Longstreet's Assault. After the Confederate defeats on July 2nd, it is Robert E. Lee's idea to push his center forward against the Union center, hoping to amass enough firepower at the Union center to break through and expand the gap in the line, thereby cutting the Union battle line in half. Lee gives that order to James Longstreet, who commands a third of Lee's army and is Lee's most trusted lieutenant—especially after the death of Stonewall Jackson in May of 1863. It is Longstreet who puts this plan together. He places 13,000 men in battle line to assault the Union center. He also arranges for 152 Confederate cannons to fire at the Union center and weaken it prior to the Confederate assault.

We are also on the position of Edward Porter Alexander, a 28-year old major in the Confederate artillery, who is given the awesome task of placing at least 70

GEORGE E. PICKETT, CSA

JAMES LONGSTREET, CSA

Confederate cannons to fire on the Union center. Alexander is also given the responsibility of determining when the Union center is weak enough to be attacked. His artillery line starts about where we are right now, and his 70 guns, covering Pickett's division, stretch out here to our right. You can see the guns in the distance in front of that white building out there (the Klingle Farm). Alexander's artillery line pretty much parallels the Emmitsburg Road to our right (to the right of Big Round Top, which you see in the distance). The signal guns that begin the attack are next to the Klingle Farm, and just to the right of the white house (an original structure) are two more guns, which begin one of the greatest artillery duels in American history.

EDWARD P. ALEXANDER, CSA

Another 63 cannons, from A. P. Hill's Corps, are pushed out of the tree line into the open fields beyond. Yet another ten guns from Richard Ewell's artillery are placed well north of Gettysburg (where the college stands today). It's interesting to note that, when the attack begins, some of the most effective fire comes from that area. Ewell and his commanders have no idea what they are hitting, but they fire over the town, aiming at anything on the Union battle line. Some of the most effective fire takes place from Ewell in the north, but he only fires for 10-15 minutes when the artillery barrage begins. The main artillery barrage continues for an hour and forty-five minutes.

A. P. HILL, CSA

Robert E. Lee has decided he will attack the Union center (that clump of trees you see directly in front of you, just to the left of the obelisk monument to the Army of the Potomac). Because any advance across these fields will be a smoky affair, the Confederates look for something on the horizon to aim at, and they aim at that clump of trees. Now those are not the original trees, but they are the descendants of the original trees. Lee knows this is not going to be easy; he's not stupid. There are still 6,000 Union soldiers in multiple lines along that ridgeline in a 300-yard front. There are also 122 Union cannons from Cemetery Hill (to your left, just on the other side of the town—those trees that you see to your left), down along the ridge line in front of us, and well to the right to the smaller of the two hills that you see to your right, which is Little Round Top. Then 122 Union cannons start firing at the Confederate infantry as soon as they move into these fields, following their own cannonade.

The Confederate cannonade begins first. At one o'clock in the afternoon, two guns from Miller's Battery—the Louisiana battery under the command of Captain Merritt B. Miller—signal the beginning of one of the great cannonades in American history. One hundred and fifty-two Confederate cannons start firing at the Union center. One hundred and twenty-two Union cannons fire back. That makes 274 cannons firing at each other for nearly two hours. The sound was so incredibly loud they could hear it in the streets of Baltimore and Washington, D.C. In fact, sound engineers in the 1970s determined that it was the loudest man-made sound ever heard on the North American continent until they exploded the atomic bomb in New Mexico in July of 1945.

Originally the cannonade is supposed to last for only 20-45 minutes, but it lasts for an hour and 45 minutes. Conservatively, the artillery barrage begins about one o'clock and is over just slightly before 3:00 PM. Actually it is stopped by the Union commander, Henry Hunt, who is very, very worried that the valley is filling up with so much smoke that the Confederates could burst out of that smoke to surprise the Union position. Therefore he starts ordering his batteries to cease-fire approximately 10-15 minutes before the Confederates cease firing themselves. At 3:00 PM, the guns grow silent.

Ten minutes later one of the more magnificent sights of the entire American Civil War occurs when 13,000 Confederates emerge from the tree line behind you. On our left (past this fence line and past that first line of trees where you can just see some open high ground on your left) is the formation of James Pettigrew's division. Right behind Pettigrew and slightly to the left is Isaac Trimble's division of Confederates. Those units constitute the left flank of what we call Pickett's Charge, or Longstreet's Assault.

HENRY J. HUNT, USA

On our right here is Pickett's division. In the wood line (Spangler Woods) is Louis Armistead's command. In fact, the 38th Virginia (his left-most regiment) is pretty close to the Virginia worm fence, which you can see today along the park path leading toward the Virginia Memorial. About 200 yards in front of Armistead and slightly to his right (in this slight ravine in front of us) is Richard Garnett's brigade. His right-most regiment is just about in front of that red barn (the Spangler Farm). From the Spangler Farm (even farther to the right, heading down to that park tower in the distance) is the right flank of George Pickett's division, James Kemper's brigade. Even farther to the right and rear (which should have been Pickett's right flank support) are David Lang's Florida brigade and what is left of Cadmus Wilcox's Alabama brigade.

At three o'clock the cannonade ends. Ten minutes later, 13,000 Confederates emerge from this tree line. As soon as they appear, the 122 Union cannons start firing at them from Cemetery Hill to Little Round Top.

One of the best things, in my opinion, that the park has done in many, many years is to put that fence up. That fence pretty much separates the two halves of Pickett's Charge. It's the type of fence that would have been there—a four-foot split rail fence. It indicates that the ground in front of us is not as flat as it looks, but has quite a few undulations that play an important part in the Confederate advance across this field.

We call this Pickett's Charge, but these men do not charge across the field. It is 87 degrees and humid, their guns weigh nine pounds, and they have been pounded by the artillery barrage—the overshoots of the artillery on both sides—for quite a while. It is a miserable atmosphere to start moving through these open fields. We're 1,275 yards away from the Union position, but many of these Confederates have well over a mile to travel. Now, they do not charge across this field; they march across at common time, which is 90 steps to the minute with a stride of 28 inches (that's about as fast as you and I walk from one place to another). It takes 18 minutes for most of the Confederates to cross this field under fire every step of the way.

Fortunately, however, the Confederates have these undulations (marked by this fence) to help them stay out of the frontal fire from the Union artillery. However, they are not able to take cover from the flanking fire coming from the Union cannons on Cemetery Hill and Little Round Top which is hitting obliquely into their ranks. There's a great attrition rate between this point and the Emmitsburg road, which is about 250 yards in front of the Union position. It's at that point that 6,000 Union infantry in multiple lines began firing at the Confederates. That's when many of those Union cannons along the ridgeline directly in front of the Confederate advance began firing their canister, as well.

There is one story that should be noted here. Robert E. Lee has envisioned that the entire Union battle line will be ablaze. He is not able to succeed in that vision for one very good reason. In the morning and early in the afternoon of July 3rd, the Union soldiers dictate the schedule with their attacks against the lower portion of Culp's Hill and the Union cavalry build-up against the Confederate right flank. Lee is well aware that the Confederates need artillery support during this advance, and he selects nine howitzers. Now a howitzer is like a mortar with its very high trajectory. Lee decides that nine howitzers should move forward with the advancing column. When the infantry and cannons get halfway into this field, they will unlimber, turn their guns around, and give artillery support to the Confederate effort at the Union center.

One of the remarkable aspects of the American Civil War is that the Confederate army (at least in the East) does not like to move forward under its own artillery fire because of faulty fuses. These fuses have such a nasty habit of blowing up prematurely that the Confederates are always looking over their shoulders when their own artillery is firing over their heads. They don't mind mortars, however, because of the high trajectory. Even if a mistake should take place with a mortar, the airburst is well above their heads. Thus the Confederates don't mind the idea of moving forward with nine howitzers. These are called Poague's Howitzers, after an artillery commander from A. P. Hill's Corps—Major William T. Poague. Poague places howitzers very close behind what is now the Virginia Memorial (where Lee is sitting on his horse, Traveler).

Unfortunately, those guns do not move forward for one very good reason. The entire Confederate artillery is under the command of William Pendleton, one of Robert E. Lee's good friends. There is a great deal of overshoot (some historians believe as much as 60%), killing a lot of cooks and ambulance drivers but not hitting the Union position they were trying to soften up for the infantry assault. There is also considerable Union overshoot, as well. Many of those cannon blasts fall among Pickett's division (on your right), especially into Kemper's Brigade (down near Spangler Woods). They are right behind Dearing's guns, as you can see. Much of the Union overshoot is falling near the ammunition train and the nine howitzers that are directly behind where Lee's Monument stands today.

WILLIAM PENDLETON, CSA

Consequently, William Pendleton, without telling E. P. Alexander or any of A. P. Hill's Corps, has moved the train, on his own initiative, about a quarter of a mile due west of its position. As a result, when these batteries start to run dry on ammunition and the artillery commanders start looking for more ammunition to support their infantry, they do not find it. Similarly, when these nine howitzers are needed for the advance, they find those nine howitzers and the ammunition train have been moved by Pendleton a quarter of a mile behind the lines. Thus no ammunition can be dispersed to these artillery pieces in the form of reserve, especially if there is a Union counter-charge. They have nothing left except short-range ammunition (canister), and the nine howitzers do not move forward with the infantry.

As a result, when the Confederates step off from this position, moving across the field at common time, there is no artillery support for them. There are 122 Union cannons firing at the Confederates as they move across the field, and when the Confederates get about half-way across, the Union sharpshooters from Cemetery Ridge start firing—un-horsing and downing as many officers as they see in their sights. When the Confederates finally reach the fences along the Emmitsburg Road, the 6,000 Union infantry in a 300-yard front start firing at them. That will be our next position.

CANNONBALL

THE COPSE OF TREES FROM THE EMMITSBURG ROAD

The events described in this tour occurred in the
Afternoon, July 3, 1863

Emmitsburg Road ∾

BLOOD POOLS BY ROADSIDE FENCES AS UNION CANNONS FIRE ON PICKETT'S STALLED MEN

The Confederates come across this field behind us (where you can see Robert E. Lee aboard his horse, Traveler). Two Confederate columns—James Pettigrew's division and Isaac Trimble's division) move across these open fields on the other side of this fence line, and they are angling in this direction. To your right (where you see a red barn in the distance), James Kemper's brigade is moving in at a severe angle. At the Klingle Farm (the white building to your right), Kemper's Brigade crosses the road, then angles, coming parallel to the road (just before it reaches the Codori Farmhouse, the red barn and farmhouse to our right) and then attacks the Union center (directly in front of us).

JAMES L. KEMPER, CSA

As you can see, the Confederates are angling at this point quite severely, and those flanking brigades are suffering the worst because of the Union artillery fire from both flanks. A number of cannons on Cemetery Hill (just off to our left front) are firing into the left flank of Pettigrew's and Trimble's brigades as they move toward the Union center. From Little Round Top, there is a line of Union artillery under the command of Brigadier General James Hunt. Hunt has spread his artillery reserve from the Pennsylvania Memorial to the base of Little Round Top, all angling in this direction. That means the flanking brigades of both halves of Pickett's Charge (Longstreet's Assault) are getting mauled quite badly by Union artillery as they come across this field. However, the worst is yet to come.

As the Confederates advance toward this road, there are 6,000 Union soldiers in multiple lines along the ridge-line directly in front of you—that's Cemetery Ridge. Those men have been told to hold their fire until the

Confederates reach the fences along the Emmitsburg Road. There are two five-foot fences, one on either side of the road that the Confederates cannot knock down. They were built by German Mennonites, and if you know anything about the Mennonites, you know that they build things to last forever. The postholes along the road were said to be as much as two feet deep. When the Confederates reach these fences, which they expect to be able to push down just by the weight of their numbers, they can not. They have to go up and over one fence into the roadbed and then up and over another fence.

Unfortunately for them, 6,000 Union infantry are now ordered to open up and start firing. At the same time, dozens of Union cannons directly in front of the Confederate advance switch to canister or double charges of canister. Canister is a tin can holding 26 to 30 one-inch iron balls packed with sawdust. When you place canister in any type of cannon—either Napoleons (the green cannons you see on the battlefield) or rifled cannons (the black cannons)—with two-and-a-half pounds of gunpowder and ignite the gunpowder, the can ruptures in the muzzle. Then, like a giant shotgun, these 26 to 30 one-inch iron balls come flying at you. They say that one of those balls can cut a man in half at 500 yards, yet the Confederates keep coming.

At this point, the amount of fire is so great that the Confederate advance stalls along the road while the soldiers get up and over both fences. To give you an idea of the amount of fire being directed at the Confederate advance, the park has on display an original piece of the fence line. It's three inches wide and nearly eight feet long; it has 268 bullet holes in it! There are heaps of dead Confederates on either side of the two fences, and there is so much Confederate blood on the Emmitsburg Road that it pools into low areas along the sides of the road. Still the Confederates keep coming.

To give you an idea of the carnage on the road, the Union army buried 522 dead Confederates here after the battle. Because of the incredible amount of fire, many Confederates take cover in the road and go no farther. They have to be prodded by their officers. At this point you can hear Confederate officers yelling at their men, "Home is over the next ridge, boys!"—meaning, if they can break the line in front of them, the two years of privations that they have suffered are over and they might just win this war.

There is no way to place the Confederates in battle line from the Emmitsburg Road to the first Union positions along the west wall (the first line of defense, where you see the first line of monuments). The men all mingle together, and they go forward for their own reasons. Many historians believe that the last 200 yards of this charge are simply an exercise in Confederate courage and commitment. When you consider the volume of fire of the Union soldiers and the cannons, these men go forward, not because they are ordered to do so, but under their own volition. They go because of their own pride, demonstrating their courage and commitment.

The Confederates, in fact, re-form their lines the best they can when they get to the other side of both fences, and then they start moving forward. They are still not at a run and do not start charging with bayonets fixed until they are halfway between the road and the first Union battle line (60 yards in front of the Union position along the visual crest of the ridge that you see there).

The first two Confederate brigades that engage at the angle are B. D. Fry's Tennesseans and Alabamans. Colonel Fry has taken over when General Archer was captured by the Iron Brigade on July 1st. Colonel Fry's men and Richard Garnett's men reach the Union position first, and they engage at the stone wall for about five minutes. Coming up directly behind them are two more of George Pickett's division—Louis Armistead's brigade on the left and James Kemper's brigade on the right. They hit the Union battle line with the remnants of four brigades and break the first line of defense at the west wall. They drive what is left of the Union position (that first initial advance position) back about 60 yards into the main Union battle line at the visual crest of Cemetery Ridge.

RICHARD B. GARNETT, CSA

Now, when the Confederates first emerge from the wood line, their battle line is at least a mile in length, stretching from the middle of that high ground (to your right), well to the left (past Lee's statue), past Pickett's division (Armistead and Garnett), well past Kemper's Brigade (past that red barn). Halfway between that red barn and that tower (way in the distance) is Pickett's immediate support on his right flank—David Lang's Florida brigade and Cadmus Wilcox's Alabama brigade. Those men do not step off at the same time as all the other Confederates do. They start out about 15 minutes into the advance. Unfortunately, they are not told that the entire Confederate effort is converging on one central point (this clump of trees). They move almost directly forward, so that with every step they take, they move farther away from Pickett, removing his flank support.

When the Confederates first advance from the wood line behind us, the battle line is a little more than a mile in length from flank to flank. When they finally hit the Union battle line and break the first line of defense, they are compressed into a 300-yard front. Stretched on our left from those white buildings (the Brian Farm) to our right (the obelisk monument), is the right flank of Kemper's Brigade (the right flank of Pickett's division). Well to our right (heading toward the Pennsylvania Memorial that you see in the distance) are David Lang's and Cadmus Wilcox's brigades. They have been stopped almost entirely by artillery fire before being driven back, so they can offer no support whatsoever to Pickett's right flank during this assault.

You have one mile of Confederates being compressed into a 300-yard front called a "massed column assault." There is nothing wrong with a "massed column assault" as long as it keeps on rolling; but when it stops, it becomes a huge target because of its density. If you are a Union soldier firing into that mass of Confederates, all you have to do is fire in that direction, and you will hit someone. A "massed column assault" is only good if it acts as a steamroller; but if you stop, you become a huge target. That's exactly what takes place here. Once the Confederates are successful at the stone wall, their advance stops, they go aground temporarily, and then they get shot to pieces.

FENCES ON THE EMMITSBURG ROAD

THE COPSE OF TREES FROM THE ANGLE

The events described in this tour occurred in the
Afternoon, July 3, 1863

The Angle

PICKETT'S CHARGE CULMINATES AT THE BLOODY ANGLE

We're at the Union center on July 3rd—the target of one of the great military charges in American history, known as Pickett's Charge. This really should be called the Pickett-Pettigrew-Trimble Assault because all three divisions were involved. Even more accurately, it should be called Longstreet's Assault because it was James Longstreet who put this together under Lee's orders.

What you see in the distance—the monument of Robert E. Lee on his horse Traveler—is the position where Lee viewed the action on that July 3rd (in that little wooded cul-de-sac). The Confederates fire from this position for nearly two hours (1:00-3:00 PM) with 152 Confederate cannons that are pushed out of the tree line that you see in front of you. From the Union side, 122 cannons answer. That's 274 cannons firing at each other for nearly two hours. At three o'clock the guns grow silent.

Ten minutes later, 13,000-15,000 Confederates emerge from the tree line in front of you. Their battle line stretches well over a mile (literally from horizon to horizon, from right to left). The reason we have a discrepancy in the numbers is because there are about 13,000 Confederates who converge to attack this position. If we add the two brigades supporting George Pickett's division on the right flank (David Lang's Florida brigade and Cadmus Wilcox's Alabama brigade), then there are 15,000 men.

Lang's and Wilcox's brigades do not advance until 15 minutes after Pickett's division begins, so they always trail. In fact, they never reach Pickett's right flank. Look in the distance, past the Codori Farmhouse, up the Emmitsburg Road, to the white picket fence at the Rodgers Farm. Wilcox and Lang go right through there, across these fields to where the Pennsylvania Memorial now stands today. That position is well away from the right flank of George Pickett's division, which is just this side of this Virginia worm fence (this stockade fence to our left front).

As soon as the Confederates move out of this tree line, 122 Union cannons start firing at them, and the Confederates pay for every foot they move across this field. There's the Emmitsburg Road with the two five-foot fences—the Confederates call them the "damned Yankee fences"—built by German Mennonites. Some of those postholes go down as far as two feet, and when the Confederates reach those fences, they can't knock them down, so they have to go up and over both fences. It is at that point that Union soldiers—6,000 of them compressed in a 300-yard front—open up. That's also when dozens of Union cannons began to fire double charges of canister.

Still the Confederates keep coming. When they get halfway across this field—between that fence in the distance and this wall in front of us, the West Wall—the Confederates give their famous Rebel yell and charge the advance Union position—1,600 men from the Philadelphia Brigade who are manning this forward position. Their commander (you can see his monument over your shoulder), Brigadier General Alexander Webb, is awarded the Congressional Medal of Honor for his actions in defense of the Union center that day.

Two Confederate brigades hit this position at about the same time—Richard Garnett's brigade (the left-most flank of Pickett's Division), and Archer's Brigade (now under the command of Colonel B.D. Fry, after Archer is captured on July 1st by the Iron Brigade). Fry's target is this clump of trees (over our left shoulder). The two Confederate brigades hit the Philadelphia brigade almost at the same time. A hand-to-hand fight ensues for about five minutes, and it is a Confederate success. They cause 500 Union casualties and drive a fair percentage of what is left of the Union soldiers from this forward position.

ALEXANDER S. WEBB, USA

These Union soldiers fall back about 60 yards into the main Union battle line (right behind us, where that road is today). Once the Confederates achieve their success at this wall, their advance stops, going to ground temporarily.

At this point, the Union commands swing around both flanks of the Confederate advance. On our left you can see an obelisk monument in the distance with a man silhouetted against the sky on the top. That's Brigadier General George Stannard of Vermont, who has been ordered by Winfield Scott Hancock to move two regiments—the 13th and 16th Vermont—forward into these open fields to enfilade (fire into) the right flank of George Pickett's division.

The same thing happens against the Confederate left flank. Look toward the motel, where there's a little monument to the 8th Ohio under the command of Lieutenant Colonel Franklin Sawyer. Sawyer does the very same thing. On his own initiative, Sawyer swings down Cemetery Ridge and fires into the left flank of the Confederates—Pettigrew's division and then Trimble's brigades. New York and New Jersey troops do the same. The Confederates find themselves in a box—a "double envelopment"—being fired at from the front and now from both sides. They are shot to pieces.

GEORGE J. STANNARD, USA

Fortunately two more Confederate brigades now hit this position. They are the brigades of James Kemper, who has obliqued dramatically (from the Rodgers Farm, just to the left of the Codori Farmhouse) and Louis Armistead (to Kemper's left and across the road directly in front of us). They join what is left of Garnett's and Fry's brigades at this wall, where they still have 60 yards to break the Union battle line.

Some Confederate officer has to lead these men on before they are completely shot to pieces. Brigadier General Louis Armistead takes his hat off, puts it on the tip of his sword, and, charging through his men to this wall, faces his troops and yells, "Come on, boys, let's give them the cold steel! Who will follow me?" Armistead charges across this wall toward the guns behind us. At least 150 men charge with him, but they don't get very far. That monument that you see with a lot of dirt around its base marks the spot

FRANKLIN SAWYER, USA

where Louis Armistead—that very brave Confederate general—is shot down. There is some controversy about the exact position where Armistead is wounded. It's anywhere between this monument and the stone wall, and it's probably closer to the stone wall. Armistead dies two days later of wounds received.

LOUIS A. ARMISTEAD, CSA

The 150 men who charge with him don't get much farther. They probably get to these guns before they are shot back. When Armistead goes down, his 150 men are charging in this direction. When they get to about where we're standing, thousands of Union soldiers behind us (along the visual crest of Cemetery Ridge) open up on them. Those Confederates are shot to pieces. The rest of the Confederates, viewing this through all the smoke, look behind them to see if Lee is sending any support. When they see no support being sent, they start backing away from the position. Their retreat, however, is almost as bad as the advance. Many of the Union outfits countercharge those "damned Yankee fences" along the Emmitsburg Road, killing, wounding, and capturing an additional 2,000 Confederates.

The advance, attack, and retreat of Pickett's Charge take just 50 minutes. In those 50 minutes the Confederates lose nearly 7,500 men in the effort. Of the 6,000 Union soldiers defending only 300 yards (just this side of the Vermont Monument, and over to the Brian Farm) nearly 2,500 are killed, wounded, or captured.

This is the climax of the battle. This is Lee's last chance to poke a hole in the Union battle line—possibly the last good chance the Confederate army has to bring about an end to this war in their favor. In these fields of Pickett's Charge, in 50 minutes, you have nearly 10,000 American casualties. The gentleman over our right shoulder is George Gordon Meade, the Union commander at Gettysburg, sitting on his horse, Baldy. His monument stands approximately a mile from the statue of Robert E. Lee sitting on his horse, Traveler. That'll give you a pretty good idea how far the Confederates would have to go to breach the Union battle line. For this charge to be successful, they would have had to expand the gap laterally.

Robert E. Lee remains in his battle lines for almost 24 more hours after Pickett's Charge, hoping that George Gordon Meade will make the same mistake that he did the day before by advancing across these open fields. When Meade does not oblige, Lee, in a driving rainstorm late in the afternoon of July 4th, decides to pick up his marbles and head back to Virginia. He retreats across those mountains reaching the valleys on the other side, then turns south (to your left), finally crossing the Potomac River on July 14th, and ending the Gettysburg Campaign.

The three-day battle at Gettysburg—July 1st, 2nd, and 3rd, 1863—resulted in 51,000 American casualties: 23,000 Union and 28,000 Confederate. That's 11,000 dead (approximately 5,500 on each side), 26,000 wounded that did recover, and 14,000 captured or listed as missing in action. Of those men captured and sent to prison camp, one in every five would die in prison camp. This was the greatest conflagration in the history of the North American continent, and it ended with one of the great charges in military history.

ABRAHAM LINCOLN DEDICATES THE SOLDIER'S NATIONAL CEMETERY

The events described in this tour occurred in the
July 10 - November 19, 1863

National Cemetery

FINAL RESTING PLACE OF 3,512 UNION DEAD DEDICATED BY ABRAHAM LINCOLN

We're standing in the National Cemetery. This is the final resting place of 3,512 Union dead in the battle. It was dedicated just four-and-a-half months after the Battle of Gettysburg by the 16th President of the United States, Abraham Lincoln. Lincoln dedicated these 17 acres with a very simple speech called the Gettysburg Address. The cemetery is arranged in 18 sections representing the 18 states that fought in the Union army here at Gettysburg. It also comprises two sections of Union unknown.

ABRAHAM LINCOLN

The monument that you see directly in front of you is the Soldier's National Monument. Most visitors believe (in fact we lead them to believe), that it is the approximate location where the Gettysburg Address was given. However, the platform, which was about 12' x 20', on which Lincoln gave the Gettysburg Address, was probably closer to the Evergreen Cemetery (the town cemetery). Evergreen Cemetery is just on the other side of that wrought iron fence that you see in the distance. That's probably where the lectern was. In fact, Lincoln would have been facing us when he delivered his speech.

The reason for building the cemetery was actually quite obvious. On July 10th, just a few days after the Battle of Gettysburg, the War Governor of the State of Pennsylvania, Andrew Curtin, came to Gettysburg to view the carnage. He was given a tour of this battlefield by a 32-year old attorney by the name of David Wills. What the Governor of Pennsylvania saw sickened him. There were 8,900 men who died on the field without seeing a doctor. Two thousand more died at Gettysburg hospitals over the next 60 days. The majority of the 8,900 men who died of terrible wounds on this battlefield were pretty much buried where they fell.

Right after the Battle of Gettysburg, there were days of rain that washed out the graves. There were puddles with arms and legs and skulls sticking out of the mud. Also there were about 800 turkey vultures that descended on this battlefield. Then tens of millions of green-headed flies descended. The only farm animals in the area that had not been run off by either army were the giant hogs. They were too heavy to carry and too slow to move along with the armies. These giant hogs were unearthing the bodies and feeding off them. These sights sickened Governor Curtin.

He really didn't give a tinker's damn about the Confederates down on this battlefield, but he did care about the Union dead. Governor Curtin commissioned David Wills to purchase some property and start reburying the Union dead as soon as possible into more permanent gravesites. The success of the project was literally assured when the Union Provost Marshall of Gettysburg—Colonel Henry C. Almond—issued an order in the last week of July prohibiting any further exhuming of bodies and shipping them home. He feared the pestilence they might incur.

You have to understand that, by three weeks after the Battle of Gettysburg, these bodies were so badly decomposed, when they were filled with embalming fluid, the fluid came right out of their backs because the veins had broken down. This situation was clearly a health hazard. As a result, anyone who had not claimed family members up to that point had two choices—either wait until the first frost (October 25th that year), or start reburying the bodies here. By the end of July, Wills had purchased, for the cost of $2,475.87, the 17 acres that are now the National Cemetery.

Late in August of 1863, William Saunders was charged by David Wills, the architect of the cemetery, with a budget of $35,000 to landscape and lay out the cemetery. Frederick W. Biesecker was the lowest bidder to start reburying the bodies from their temporary graves on the battlefield to this location. The low bid was $1.59 per body. Biesecker's people waited until the first frost—October 25th that year. On October 26th the first body—Enoch Endetti, an Ohioan—was re-interred from the field to the cemetery. They continued burying about 60 bodies a day until November 19th, the day of the Dedication of the Cemetery by Lincoln. By the time Lincoln gave the Gettysburg Address, almost 1,400 Union dead had been reburied from their temporary graves on the battlefield to this location. Not only did Lincoln have about 15,000 people listening to his words, he was addressing, as well, the Union dead who lay in the cemetery.

The largest section in this cemetery is for the state of New York. In fact, there were more New Yorkers killed here at Gettysburg than those from any other state. That's why the New York State Memorial to our left was placed here; it's a place of honor. The section directly on your left is the New York section, with 867 New Yorkers buried there.

Invitations were sent to all the War Governors of the 18 states, as well as generals George Gordon Meade and Winfield Scott. Edward Everett of Massachusetts, one of the most famous orators of the day, was invited to speak here, but he could not make the date that was originally scheduled (October 23rd). Then. Everett said he could probably make November 19th, and that date was accepted by the other participants, including Lincoln and his Cabinet, who were invited as an afterthought to give "a few appropriate remarks."

Edward Everett spoke here on the platform for almost two hours. He compared Gettysburg to the Peloponnesian War. He dealt with almost every aspect of the battle and was given a thunderous ovation. After two hours he sat down. Then, with 15,000 people in attendance, Abraham Lincoln stood up and, in his tenor voice, began a very simple speech of 272 words. It lasted about two minutes, but even after being interrupted five times by applause, he did not think it was that great a speech. He thought he had failed. Lincoln stayed to listen to the rest of the program, with his head hung low. Then Edward Everett came over and said, "Mr. President, you said in two minutes what I couldn't say in two hours"—and he was right. Probably the greatest understatement in American history is when Lincoln said, "The world will little note, nor long remember, what we say here...," but in that same sentence, he continued, "but it can never forget what they did here."

EDWARD EVERETT

❧ The Gettysburg Address ❧

◆ NOVEMBER 19, 1863 ◆
DEDICATORY REMARKS OF PRESIDENT LINCOLN
AT THE CONSECRATION OF
THE SOLDIER'S NATIONAL CEMETERY

Four score and seven years ago our fathers brought forth on this continent, a new nation, conceived in Liberty, and dedicated to the proposition that all men are created equal. Now we are engaged in a great civil war, testing whether that nation, or any nation so conceived and so dedicated, can long endure. We are met on a great battle-field of that war. We have come to dedicate a portion of that field, as a final resting place for those who here gave their lives that that nation might live. It is altogether fitting and proper that we should do this.

But, in a larger sense, we can not dedicate—we can not consecrate—we can not hallow this ground. The brave men, living and dead, who struggled here, have consecrated it, far above our poor power to add or detract. The world will little note, nor long remember what we say here, but it can never forget what they did here. It is for us the living, rather, to be dedicated here to the unfinished work which they who fought here have thus far so nobly advanced. It is rather for us to be here dedicated to the great task remaining before us—that from these honored dead we take increased devotion to that cause for which they gave the last full measure of devotion—that we here highly resolve that these dead shall not have died in vain—that this nation, under God, shall have a new birth of freedom—and that government of the people, by the people, for the people, shall not perish from the earth.

PHOTOGRAPHS COURTESY OF:
GARY KROSS COLLECTION
STEPHEN RECKER COLLECTION
GETTYSBURG NATIONAL MILITARY PARK
LIBRARY OF CONGRESS
NATIONAL ARCHIVES
U.S. ARMY HISTORY INSTITUTE

SPECIAL THANKS TO:
ANTIGONI & EVERETT LADD,
TIGRETT CORP.

ART DIRECTION & DESIGN:
DAN PARSONS

ADDITIONAL DESIGN & PRODUCTION:
TOM COLANDREA